AF527315

Me To Mommee

Aarti Bhatia

Copyright © 2019 by Aarti Bhatia.

All rights reserved. No part of this publication may be reproduced, distributed, or transmitted in any form or by any means, including photocopying, recording, or other electronic or mechanical methods, without the prior written permission of the publisher, except in the case of brief quotations embodied in critical reviews and certain other non commercial uses permitted by copyright law. For permission requests, write to the publisher address.

Any references to historical events, real people, or real places are based on the author's own experiences. Other names, characters, places, and events are products of the author's imagination, and any resemblances to actual events or places or persons, living or dead, are entirely coincidental.

Edited by Aditi Bhatt

Cover by Malhar Tanna

Published by Outliers Publishing Pvt. Ltd.

First Edition 2019

ISBN: 978-81-942684-1-3

Dedication

It is surprising to see how three words stand to capture a trunk full of memories that define my journey of motherhood.

It began with the search for an email address; I wanted to secure one for my newborn girl. This was the ongoing trend that one may write to the future of their child, telling them if & how wonderfully their childhood panned out.

I couldn't find the id I sought for my child.
So I decided to write a blog, with the same effect – letterstopiya.blogspot.com

While I had seen & experienced the bluer side of young motherhood called post-partum-blues, I was determined to rediscover the brighter side of the same as I captured events that made my world spin a little slower around my darling baby.

It is heart-warming to see in retrospect how that one decision changed the course of my writing.

It is also surprising to see how I managed to jot it down at all!

It was tough to keep writing to my child with consistency. All of my day went into feeding & cleaning her. And for the remaining amount of time, I used to find myself too out of breath to even pick up a pen, let alone write something.

But I knew this – as fast as a little one grows up, every day brings something new into a mother's life; I was witnessing it first hand.
If I did not register an adorable moment the same day it happened, I would have to rely on fading memories to tell me of the glory of this phase of motherhood.

As funny as it may sound, I have written most of these chapters on the keypad of my cell phone.

I used to wait for some quiet in the night to come, which wasn't easy as my baby was not an early-to-bed-kind-of-child. But once she was asleep, I used to drag my fatigued body up, click open my cell phone and write. It wasn't much hard after that as once I got down to putting words to the day's events, a smile was hard to evade. All of my tiredness used to melt into the warmth in my chest, as I recalled the delight of being with my child, through the lens of my letters.

It was some time later that I realized how wonderfully universal these feeling I was trying to capture are!

The blog gained an audience in the mothers in my social circle. I started receiving comments over how relatable my words were for any & every mother!

I overjoyed at having placed feelings well through words.

It was exciting to create new friendships through a common feeling called baby-love.

A little over a year into writing, as well as sharing, my letters within friends & family, I got the last push from my husband to make my captures reach a larger audience. (Much love to him for that.)

Within the small social circle that I had developed so far, I reached out to Dr. Falguni Vasavada. A professor by profession, a mentor to many and a body-positive fashionista, she was all that I hoped for – encouragingly helpful & how!

She got me in touch with the woman who has put her faith in me & my book, Bhavini Mehta, my publisher.

And the rest, I hope, will be history.
I owe a big, fat hug (and then many more of these) to my muse, my baby, Piya, who has unknowingly helped me script this book to near-perfection.

With a lot of gratitude towards my family, mentors & friends, I am publishing this book with the hope that it finds a friend in women across the globe, just as I wish they do the same in 'Me to Mommee'.

Me to Mommee

- A Concept Book By Aarti Bhatia

The first touch of your child's tiny fingers on your skin. The beautiful red pout their lips made while trying to say 'Agooooo'. The comforting hug of their super tiny, cottony-soft romper around their body and, through that, around your arms.

The blissful sleep your child had after nourishing from a stomach full of your milk.
The beat your heart skipped when your little one yawned. The tremendous amount of strength you had to muster to stop yourself from kissing your adorable infant a million times in their sleep, because God knows you did not want to wake them up!

And to then sit wondering how the days passed by without allowing you enough time to revel in this phase called 'Baby Bliss'.

Feelings are hard to put words to, when they are this precious!

This book is a small attempt from one mother to express such memorable experiences of every mother.

It will tell you of the nights spent in sleeplessness. It will tell you of the days spent in playfulness. It will tell you of the moments that ought to be cherished forever. And it will tell you of the tough times that one should happily remember.

But mostly, it will tell you 'Yes, this happened to me too! Such is the tale of every Mother!'

Lastly, it will be the best possible memoir for your child, who is as much a part of this journey of motherhood as you have been; let them know how wonderful these times are, how much you want to hold onto the fleeting days of their innocent childhood and how loved they are & will always hence be.

This book will be your go-to best friend, almost as if you were writing it to your kid, yourself!

For expecting mothers, here is my love telling you that something brilliant awaits you in life. For new mothers, here is my gift addressed to the wonder woman in you. And for mothers who wish to relive those days of pure joy when their now-grown-up-child was just a foot tall, I hope this book makes you shed a tear or two in happiness.

As for your darling baby – along with reading them 1-2 chapters out of this book & smiling alongside at the end of a tiring day, you can also jot down similar experiences of yours, in the space provided for your thoughts. Club the parts together at the end & make a customized keepsake as a special memoir-gift for them.

Now turn over & let the amazement begin!

TABLE OF CONTENTS

One

A midnight meltdown

Giving birth to a child comes with a lot of changes in a parent's life.

For better or worse, it is the mother who tends to have a major role during the first stage of the baby's growth.

Many a time, it may feel like you weren't ready for this. Or that, maybe, you are the only one with such a huge amount of responsibility, as everyone else sails through their day with ease.

However, this story of feeling blue is more universal than you know of.

This is one such story. A story of a 'Midnight meltdown'.

When I started expecting my baby, a lot of things changed inside me, as did they around me. Some welcome changes were experiencing her movements within me and brimming with joyous anticipation. Other not so welcome ones were nausea and sleeplessness.

After my baby was born, the welcome factors increased tremendously in number. But while nausea left me, sleeplessness decided to extend its unwelcome stay. This, along with my baby's midnight crying, added a great deal of stress to my life, so much that I started to feel gloomy.

I was aware that this wasn't an unusual phenomenon amongst new mothers. But in this case being forewarned, sadly, was not being forearmed.

I was helpless against my infant's cries. I understood my child's helplessness, as well. For everything, ranging from hunger to a wet diaper to colic, she had only one means to express herself - crying with all her might.

Yet, I couldn't help but feel low.

On one fateful night when she started to cry again, my mind wandered to the events of my young, carefree days when I could stay awake and sleep at will, with not a care in the world.

Instead, I now had a haywire sleep-cycle combined with perennial fatigue.

That night as I reminisced all these changes, all at once, I silently thought to myself, "Life will never be the same again".

As I sat on my bed, with my sleepy baby in my arms, this thought felt like too heavy a weight for my tender emotions to bear.

I looked at my crying baby.
As her drowsy eyes caught my sight, her cries began to subside.
As if reading my mind, her eyes blended into a soft smile.

I couldn't stop myself from smiling back.
I touched her innocent face, soft as a feather.
Thinking that I was offering her something to eat, she gleefully opened her mouth in the direction of my hand. My frown immediately turned into a delightful chuckle!

As if mocking me, she started to hum with giggles too. Seeing her toothless little mouth laughing in front of me, I started feeling positive
again.

I put her head on my shoulder and I rocked her gently.

As her mellow body went weightless over mine, a warm feeling of never-experienced-before bliss filled my chest.

“Life will truly never be the same again" I thought.
This time, with a smile.

Two

A lemon tree

As long as the nights seem, after having delivered one's precious child, time sure flies by quickly.
Before you know it, your little baby has grown by a few months; and you, by a few years. Or so it would seem.
But as the dates change on the calendar, are you marking the unforgettable moments on them?

Are you marking how your heart beat the first time you held your darling child in your arms?
Or how your eyes welled up when your baby cried?
Or that time you found yourself laughing madly, after a long time, as your spouse winced at the smell of a soiled diaper?

Such stories get lost in time because your memory's film reel gets outrun by the brilliant speed of your child's growth.

This is one such story. A story of 'A lemon tree'.

Or maybe, it's a story of clouds wandering aimlessly through the sky.
My four-month-old baby did not quite specify which.

Nevertheless, I decided that four months was as good an age as any to start sharing my thoughts. I'd been doing that since she was born, by talking to her about a number of things. Till now, she had responded with a smile and some indecipherable words &sounds…Since I had no way of finding out whether she understood or agreed with my incessant talks, I'd decided to take her clueless-curiosity-filled expression as a green light to keep on talking.

Now, every mother loves the way her baby stares at things.
And since I am no different a mother, this innocent staring, I believe, is the epitome of a child's cuteness.
Be it her soft eyelashes, batting over a long stare at something as mundane as the ceiling; or a sparkling giggle-drop making way through her gaping, rosy lips – that's when I experienced what falling for someone meant.

The other day, my baby was staring out the window. She was probably looking at the lush green lemon tree in the garden, or maybe, examining the clouds making their way through the sky beyond.

Since she was really small, I kept checking on her every now and then. Eventually, I ended up mapping as well as emulating her actions. So, when she was looking up and out, I followed her curiosity. I was humbled by a

seemingly mundane, yet under-explored sight, at the same time;
Nature's marvel of green, overshadowed by a vast brush of sky blue all across it - one dancing quietly with the wind, the other pacing silently above.

Given how fast life had become, I, as an adult, had stopped making time for such "mundane" observations.

Since I could last remember, I had been tired. But, in that very moment, as I lay by my baby's side, I was more relaxed than ever.

After a minute of silent reflection, I softly thought aloud – 'This is so peaceful'.
As if agreeing with me, she immediately hummed the sound "Hmmmm".

The simple beauty of this moment stayed afloat for some time.

Breathing in, I silently wondered if my baby would grow up or if she would make a happy child out of me again. Given how wonderful her side of the world looked, I'd gladly accept the latter.

THREE

A sleepy smile to live by

As wonderful as having a baby in one's life is the initial stage of motherhood is indeed tough. In the early months, putting one's baby to sleep alone can seem like an ordeal!

And why shouldn't it? Babies exhibit an all-energetic, ready to rock & roll form, right before bedtime, don't they? This, however enjoyable for the baby, puts the mother into exhaustion, who prays that the baby goes to sleep early. But after the baby falls asleep, just looking at their pure souls sleep, can make the mother feel heavenly, however short-lived the baby's sleep be.

This is one such story. A story of 'A sleepy smile to live by'.

While my infant baby played & swayed right before bedtime, I kept trying everything in my capacity to induce sleep into her eyes, which somehow seemed to come only post 5 am. Also, it rarely lasted longer than two hours.

She did not sleep.
She took power-naps.

Eventually, this turned into a less erratic sleep-routine as time went by. But during this initial phase of dark circles under my eyes, crushing pain in my back, and throbbing ache in my head - something magical happened.

One day, at the break of dawn, when I had just put her to sleep and was about to close my eyes, I saw the very first expression of hers.

She smiled.

One second captured in a visual of her gentle sight can be described as thus:
Eyes closed.
Hands spread up & open, as if she were at gunpoint.
Legs luxuriously dangling down my lap.
Smiling.

A smile in her sleep, yet a smile bright as day,
A smile that lasted just a second, yet a smile that stayed in my memory for a life-time,
A smile to live by and a smile to die for.

I hadn't slept all night.
I couldn't have been more tired.
Yet, there I was, eyes wide open, waiting for her to give me a glimpse of that sleepy-dreamy smile of hers again.

I don't know how long I struggled to keep my droopy eyes open in hope. But I do remember falling asleep in a heavenly manner, probably smiling in sleep myself.

My baby was up in two hours, as usual. But as little as this sleep was for me, I woke up feeling refreshed.

Almost every night after that, I tried really hard to stay awake after having put her to sleep. What kept me going was the hope that I may get to see her innocent, angelic, heart-melting, sleepy-dreamy smile again.

Months have passed by since that night. She smiles much more & quite often now.
But while I cherish all of her expressions, her first smile will always be my favorite.

Jot down your thoughts

FOUR

A mother's separation anxiety

While many maternity issues have been discussed to the point of becoming repetitive, I believe some aspects have not been put into enough stories.

This is one such story. A story of 'A mother's separation anxiety'.

My child was a part of me for a long, long time.
But, by the end of that time, I kind of started to wish that my baby would come out of my womb & into my arms soon.

And then, having her in my lap felt like a dream came true!

But, it also meant that she was now no longer a part of merit's really hard to explain why this was tough to deal with.

When she was with me, inside me, I used to converse with her all the time. It was as if I was consciously aware of even my thoughts, as I felt that she was listening to them too.

She heard the same songs I did - so I chose my music very carefully.
She watched what I saw - so I dedicated time to seeing things that would generate productive impressions only.
She ate what I ate - so my meals became nutritious rather than delicious!

My point is this - during pregnancy, everything was about 'us' - her and I.
During those nine months of co-existence, I lived another short life, within this life - one with just her. I almost forgot what life outside of 'Us' was like.

And while having her play & laugh in my arms felt magical, I often caught myself doing funny things like, talking to her in my head, not realizing that she was outside of me now and that my thoughts needed to be spoken out loud for her to know them!

I know this sounds strange, but much before a child goes through separation anxiety (on the first day of school, mostly), a mother goes through it, after child birth.

Being away from her feels like being away from myself, it feels like a very important part of me is missing. That's why I love her more than anything else, because she is the most amazing part of me - more than I myself have ever been on my own.

As time goes by and she grows bigger & bigger, she will grow into the awesome, independent personality that a child is meant to be. And as much as I will love seeing that happen, our world-within-a-world phase is something I will hold close to my heart, till the end of time.

FIVE

The story of Us

When asked how motherhood feels, most mothers answer with 'It's wonderful!'

While I cannot say that I haven't used this line many times myself, I've also used its more honest variants, every once in a while.

It is really tiring, but fulfilling too.
It is very hard, but I am holding the fort somehow.
It is a sleepless, happy journey towards exhaustion.
It is a sweet & sour cookie, one I love no doubt.

I have balanced all the negatives pretty well up there, haven't I?
You laugh, but I am being nice here.

Little ones are quite a handful!

It is a task just to keep up with their constantly changing moods & preferences. The sheer creativity required to keep them entertained should qualify a mother for an award in the same regard.

Not to mention, their affinity to stay up late and keep us mothers awake alongside, as we try every trick there is to get a yawn out of them, requires supernatural energy!

Having said that, I wouldn't give up this task for the entire world.

It is taxing, yes.
Mentally and physically exhausting, yes.
Yet, I love it as much as I love cribbing about it.
It is contradictory, I know, YES!

But that is how I feel about my little girl.

Simply put -
There is nobody else in this world I would be as silly as a clown for, while falling in love with her every laugh at my goofy acts;
There is nobody I would tire my bones for, yet stand up to run again with the next minute;
There is nobody I would wish to see grow up devoid of all my flaws, while yearning to see a glimpse of me in her.

I am the one who gives my baby exasperated sighs for stubbornly denying & delaying her sleep, and consequently mine too.
And I am also the one who keeps looking at her lovely little face for a long time; as she lays asleep in my lap, while I delay putting her down, on purpose.

Just like she is the one who cries her eyes out as I pick her up from her playpen because she yearns to play some more. And she's also the one who starts crying the minute she wakes up & doesn't find me, wanting then to have my arms wrapped around her.

I am told that is what a mother-baby duo is.

Giggly & weepy, ecstatic & sad, energetic & tired, angry & confused, and doting & pleading, all at the same time.

I think I am glad that my baby & I are one such quintessential duo.

This is the story of 'Us', and may such, we always be!

SIX

Zombie or not?

A young mother's life story cannot be told without the mention of how closely new mums resemble zombies, thanks to their haywired routine. And so this is not a story of a struggle from me to mommee, but that of one between me & my zombie.

With my baby's arrival, I made a promise to myself - I would never become a zombie.

My reasons were multifold:

A. Why I had this funny thought that I could turn into a zombie, post having a baby -

While my baby kept me merrily entertained all day with rainbow-painted moments, I hardly got any time to myself.

A baby needs her mother, almost all the time, as they eat, sleep & yap all day long, leaving little to no time for the mother to herself. With my baby being no different, I just kept running around, completing my errands the minute my girl's yapping turned into napping (no matter how short-timed).

My spirit used to take a hit every time my baby started to cry just as I was to get started with the first thing on my to-do list. As this was a frequent occurrence, my face began to carry the look of a frog, bearing an awkwardly drawn pout beneath two large, sulking eyes.

I did not look good.

Hence, becoming a zombie by appearance seemed like a haunting, yet possible, occurrence.

B. Why I didn't want to turn into a zombie

If I were to turn into dark-circle-under-the-eyes, grogginess-on-the-face kind of a mother who throws her weight around due to postnatal blues, it wouldn't be unjustified.

I was raising a baby! Everything I did was justified!

Having said that, babies are sponges when it comes to absorbing everything that goes around. Everything is an object of desire to them. All memories are step-stones to a sub-conscious building for life. The formative years are most impactful on little ones.

So, I asked myself if I really wanted to paint the world as being a burden on my shoulders because of the tough tasks associated with motherhood; or colour it with the fact that I had been gifted the most stunning muse in the form of my child.

As I looked at my baby, I said to myself, "Does it have to be so hard?!" but my heart knew otherwise. Listlessness was probably all over my face.
I guess she read this, because she fixed her pupils on my dull face and following suit, she drew her eyebrows into an inquisitive-looking frown.

My eyes grew big in surprise with this, in response to which, my little copy-cat did the same!

With smile picking up on my wry lips, I inched closer and kissed her forehead.

As I moved away, she blushed and in the next moment danced her arms in the air with a lovely laughter.

If the saying 'as the company, so the colour' stands true then I will have to show my baby vibrancy in all phases of my life, to the best of my ability. I will smile more often, so that she will too.

This is how the struggle ended.
The mother in me won over the zombie I could have been.

P.S: Turning into a zombie is an expression for becoming a pale, lifeless-looking form of oneself with no enthusiasm at all. This is the final reason of why I did not, literally, turn into one.

Jot down your thoughts

SEVEN

The first-to-forever-babble

The nights seemed to have become endlessly long after my girl's birth, thanks to her unwelcome midnight vigils.

But she has sure grown up fast & how!

And as much as I've written about those times, in order to build lasting memories, there were many more beautiful events happening by the minute with her, of which only a handful have found their way to my ink.

This is one such story. A story of a child's 'First-to-forever-babble' milestone.

This is the story of the time my girl discovered the gift of voice.

I distinctly remember being really eager to hear her speak - the reasons for which were:

·Figuring out what my infant wanted was becoming a tedious game of dumb-charades
·Trying to hold myself together as she cried without reason was making me feel helpless in the face of her pain

·Trying to keep my excitement for wanting to hear her cute baby-talk was building into a strange 'Did you hear that? She just said her first word!' series of apparently 'insane' motherly claims

Then, one fine day, a few months after her birth, she finally said something that wasn't all giggles.
After that, she couldn't stop playing with sounds, trying to mouth any & every word.
It was such fun to watch her do that!

She was yet to chance upon a word that made sense, but she was really happy with what looked like the invention of a new language.
I kept trying my best to decode it, for the benefit of both of us.

Clearly, there seems to be a range of decibel-level that infants experiment with.
And so, some sounds from my baby were as soft as a kitten's mews, and some shrieks, loud enough to wake up the neighbours.
Filled with a lot of 'oooo' and 'eeee', I didn't quite get a single thing she said. And yet, it somehow felt like I had understood everything.

Then one day, soon after, she was going on 'goo-goo-gaa-gaa', I was intently looking at her. It was a moment of absolute delight.

I had nothing else on my mind but the brimming joy of seeing her explore sounds. The relaxation of forgetting everything whilst being with her was rejuvenating!

Wanting to connect with her language, I started talking to her amidst her gleeful mumbling, asking her all sorts of things.
Every once in a while, she took a pause, made eye contact and beamed with glee.
And then, suddenly she put both her hands on her cheeks and laughed at a question I'd asked.

With her small mouth gaping open and her twinkling eyes smiling at me, it seemed like I had understood her gee-gee-gaa-gaa correctly. It was almost as if she were displaying awe at me at having cracked her secret code.

It was a hurrah-moment!

I'd never enjoyed a conversation this much!
With her, even the tiniest of achievements seemed wonderful.

I spent the rest of the day hoping that she kept playing with the gift of voice to come up with new words; the existing ones are so boring that they can wait to become a part of her vocabulary.

Not to forget the joy it would bring to my heart if her first word turned out to be Mommee! This would make her father immensely jealous and there is a higher level of satisfaction attached to that.

EIGHT

A baby's firsts

When a baby comes, so does obsession with this baby, into a mother's life.
One can always find a mother going all mushy & blushy over her little one.

And what over?
The first time her baby smiled?
The first time they were able to wave?
The first time they responded to their name?
The first time they clapped their hands?
The first time they were able to sit?
Their first crawl?
Their first walk?

What is so amazing about that?
Is that not something everybody around us does?
Has anyone ever applauded an adult for being able to walk ten steps without nose-diving into the ground?

No!

Then why does it seem to inspire awe in a mother when her baby does it?
Does she think her baby wouldn't do these acts eventually?

Wouldn't her baby be an adult someday, doing all the expected chores perfectly and applause-free?

I am smiling at myself, even as I write this, just like others probably do when they see me go ga-ga over my little girl's small achievements.

There is something extraordinarily special about the firsts.
It is difficult to put that 'special' into words, but I shall try, as I tell one such story. The story of a baby's adorable first developments, or, as I like to put it, 'The Firsts'.

The Firsts count for a reason.

They build the mental album of a lifelong memorabilia, in a mother's heart.

While my bub will grow up to sit and stand with poise and even with a confident gait, I will always feel funny remembering how she wobbled from side to side the first time she tried standing up on her own.

While she may go on to learn many languages with fluency, what will tickle all my bones is the memory of me saying 'Mommee' and her repeating it as 'Mmmmmm' with fervent happiness as I hopelessly hung in there, waiting for the 'ommeeee' to come later.

While she may make dexterous use of both her hands to accomplish various tasks, I will forever cherish the first time she held a pencil in her fist, staring hard at it for long, as the discovery of movement & grip in her fingers became monumental for her realization!

As I said, there is a reason for the firsts to count. It is because they are The Firsts.

We are all in search for new & amazing things in life because after the first time, everything becomes either 'been there-done that' or a mindless routine.

While people seem to believe that motherhood puts a pause in a woman's life, it is actually quite the opposite. My life has so many firsts to keep track of; I can barely catch up with my baby's exponential development.

She will be all grown up soon and, I swear, I will miss all of this dearly.

I can't help but dwell in happiness over this phase, for now.
My baby's journey is so beautiful that the destination of adulthood can wait while she & I capture all the scenic beauty of infancy that we can.
And if that defines a mother's obsession with The Firsts, then so be it!

NINE

Nothing works!

"Nothing works!"

A new mother chants this statement more often than she says her baby's name.

This two-word response suits well as an answer to almost any query to a mother.

Let me demonstrate:

"How well does your baby sleep?"
"She doesn't. Nothing I try, works."

"What food does your baby like?"
"That always depends on her mood. Nothing I try, works."

"Why is your baby cranky?"
"Don't know. Tried everything. Nothing works."

"How are you doing?"
"Like an old vehicle. Nothing works."

That should give you a fair idea about the weightage of this phrase in my life.

Which is why this is one such story. A story of 'Nothing works!'

I grasped the importance of this statement only some days ago, though, when the following happened -

When displeased, my little baby expresses her displeasure pretty well i.e. through high-pitched wails, loud enough to defy the invention of microphones.

That day, in order to pacify my girl I put a bunch of new toys in front of her.
She loved everything almost instantly!
New toys tend to have that effect on babies, universally.

The colors fascinated her, so did the different shapes. She was finally pleased, and that meant so was I.

'Ah! So this is what works!' I thought & rejoiced, as I watched her play with glee. I felt like the hours of fatigue were sinking down my tired shoulders. I did not delay searching for a chair to sit down upon. Oh, how wonderful it was to have my back-support back. I felt relaxed...

Just for five minutes, that is.

Five minutes is what it took for her to get bored of all the toys. ALL of them!
And just like that, we were back to square one a.k.a 'Nothing Works!'
So much for 'variety is the spice of life', huh?

Then, just as I started to pack the toys away, my girl latched onto every piece she thought was being taken away from her.

And that is how I learnt the other version of this age-old adage, one applicable to babies in particular - Variety is nothing but confusing! Better stick to 'One thing at a time'.

After that day, I started introducing one toy at a time to her.
She now scrutinizes that one toy for long and only after having tested its robustness, color, texture, fragrance, taste etc. in all possible ways, does she chuck it.

And then she moves to the next, a few minutes later. The cycle of toy-play continues longer than five minutes, this way.

Meanwhile, I enjoy transient phases of:
a. 'So this is what works',
b. 'Hope the next one works' and finally,
c. 'Nothing works with this girl!'

I am held strong by the thought of that one day, when she will be a tad older – the day when after having tried a hundred different ways to convince me of something she wants, she too will get to say this –"Nothing works with Mommee!"

Till then, it's my turn.

Jot down your thoughts

TEN

A mother's cycle of life

I love my mother.
But I'd be lying if I said that this love has not grown exponentially after I became a mother myself.

Selfishly, being in 'her shoes' is more than a metaphor or a story to me now, just like mothers everywhere have told and re-told several times.

This is one such story. A story of 'A mother's cycle of life'.

It was a little past midnight.
I had put my baby to sleep.
I had some unfinished tasks to complete and was waiting to get to them as soon as my girl slept.
So I did.

What seemed like fifteen minutes of work showed up as a whopping two-hour long turn of hands on the clock!
When did the time fly by?
My child would be awake anytime now, crying with hunger, and I hadn't even gotten a few minutes of sleep yet.
I was so tired already!

'Why is this so hard?' I winced as I sat down.

Sleeping by my side, my baby started to move a little. 'Oh no, please no! Don't wake up, please!' - I pleaded in my head.

Thankfully, she settled down and I sighed in relief.

Tick tock.
Tick tock on the clock.
Why couldn't I go to sleep?
My brain was fried, and my body felt like a fallen tree, but sleep evaded me.

I started to remember how during the carefree youth days of mine, my mother used to gently run her hands through my hair and sleep would come to me like a soft hug.

Long gone were those days now.
I was no longer a kid who got gentle caressing from her mother.
I myself was a mother now.
'Would I never get to live those moments of cushioning love again?'
'Would nobody ever pamper and cuddle me now?'

As I was lost in these sleepless thoughts, my hand experienced the lightest touch ever.

My baby's tiny little fingers had sought my hand and her cotton-soft palm now rested in mine.

Before I knew it, I was fast asleep; cushioned by the love I thought would never come to me again.

What a mother was to a child once, a child was now to a mother.
Such is a mother's cycle of life.

All it takes is a gentle touch. Always.

ELEVEN

Roll over, roll over

I want to start this little piece with the rhyme -
"There were three in the bed and the little one said 'Roll over, roll over'!
So they all rolled over and one fell out!"

As you must have guessed by now, this story is about 'A baby's bed-roll-overs'.

My girl, her father and I, we three shared a bed.
And by the time my little girl started rolling over in bed, the 'one' who kept falling out of bed was her father, not me.

Till my baby started rolling over from back to tummy & vice versa, she was pretty much sedentary, kind of dependent on us for short rides in & about the house.
Now, I felt uneasy about this new development of her rolling over.
That's because she had till date ended up going to places that we, her parents, liked or chose for the sake of convenience. There was very little, if any, choice left to our baby.
Had I known of all the child-proofing hassle I would have to go through from the minute my girl started

exploring on her own, my discomfort would have come sooner.

My baby's first roll-over happened by chance.
She took a minute to absorb what had just happened and when she did, (surprise, surprise!) she started to wail.

That was just the first time, though.

As she started rolling over frequently, an exciting explorer streak in her came to surface.
She realized how much she had been missing out on so far!
She could now reach for things beyond a hand's distance. She could view things from different angles. She could even go on to invent a new metric and declare distance in terms of this new unit –'Baby-Rolls'!

"How far is the television from the bed?"
"12 baby-rolls"

"Where is my phone, honey?"
Over there, about 20 baby-rolls away…"

"What size bed-sheets do you want, Ma'am?"
"8 baby-rolls wide, please!"

If only this was as rosy for her parents too.

Don’t get me wrong, it is surely a delight to watch one’s bub twist and turn like this. But it also leaves little space for us, the parents, to sleep on the bed, since the child now lays claim upon any area reachable within their rolls. In this case, the bed in question was ours, and my daughter claimed it entirely. All of it!

As the poem goes, she rolls and rolls through the night,
asking us to 'roll over, roll over' along with her;
Which leads to her dad falling off the bed. Many times.

As the titular poem ends with only the ‘little one’ spread on the bed luxuriously, like a bed-sheet, I am probably going to be the next to fall.

Needless to say, I am dreading it with nervous anticipation.

TWELVE

A new love

When it comes to prose, there are not enough words to describe what love feels like.
Some say it feels like soft bubbles in your chest. Some believe it sounds like violins in the background of the face of your beloved. Some also think that it feels like a pause in one's heartbeat while doing a bungee jump from a cliff.

But then what does love to a young mother feel like? Ask any mother and you will be listening to stories of a lifetime.

In an attempt to capture this massive feeling, this is one such story. A story of 'A new love' - that of a mother's love.

If she is high on irritation at the messy spillage of food her baby has luxuriously indulged in, then love is the rise of powerful breaths in a mother's chest that kills her angry buzz.

If she is annoyed to no extent at her child waking up after a teenie-tiny 5-minute nap, instead of snoozing long slumber, then love is the rose in her cheeks at being kissed 'Hi!' by her little one.

If she is tired to the bone after having gathered everything her baby scattered around, for the fifteenth time, then love is the dimple in her cheek on being kissed by her baby.

Be it dark or be it bright; a mother is spellbound every time her baby looks at her.
And why not?

When a mother witnesses the adorable things her baby does, love is hard to evade.

Watching her baby splash water in the tub as she wets all the mother's clothes in the process.
Wiping her bub's mouth constantly as the baby spills more food than she swallows, creating a mushy moustache-beard on her tiny face.
Running around her little kiddo's crawling body as the baby keeps bumping into objects, with no sign of giving up.
Looking into her child's eyes and seeing her smile through the mother's tired-eye reflection

This brings me to the knowledge that happiness comes in such small packets of miraculous cuteness. At the same time, it also makes me wonder about the different theories of love, pushing me to define my own love.

I wish for a little freedom for myself as much as I fear of separation from my baby. I claim that my child is a huge part of my own self, but I also dwell in pride with every independent move she makes.
I am little selfless with her, and at the same time, a little selfish for more of her.

Instead of soft bubbles, my girl brings drooling curries out of her mouth, right into my life. Not violins, but a babbling cacophony fills our home, which I seem to not get enough of. And keeping up with my darling's pace makes bungee jumping feel like a piece of cake!

Everyone feels love differently, indeed.
It's a very integral component of one's emotions.

For me, it is this entrapment in the majestic tower of a little muse, who giggles at my captivity, as I write serenading notes to her future self.

It's safe to say that if this isn't love, then nothing is.

Jot down your thoughts

THIRTEEN

A little maze-runner

A renowned artist, Shakespeare, had said that a human being's growth trajectory usually follows this route:
Infant
School-kid
Teenager
Youth
Adult
Middle aged
Senile
Deceased

Based on my personal, day-to-day experience, I have an addition to make to these stages –

Infant
- Cranky infant
- Difficult-to-understand infant
- Impossible-to-chase infant
- Adorable-to-death infant

School kid

And so on.

Yes, I have split the first stage into four, because that's what my baby displays, not necessarily in that order, everyday. Based on that is this story. A story of 'A little maze-runner'.

While most of the crankiness and crypto-babbling is manageable, what beats me to my bones is her ever-increasing agility. It is nearly impossible to keep up with her crawls! (God help me when she starts to run).

Add the baby's inherent smartness to manoeuvre to that and I become a senile woman, panting as she chases her baby, looking way past her age.

To add trouble to my woes, we have a dining table in our home, which can be accessed from underneath - crawled under, if you may say, by my baby.
I've no doubt when I say this – even in the absence of such furniture, I am sure every baby ends up finding a place they can sneak under, away from the reach of their parent's huge body.

With my table and its chairs placed in packed-position, it had become like a maze below, the nooks & crevices of which my little girl loved exploring.

And since we have established that I had become an ageing woman post my toddler's energy-spike phase, it became awfully troublesome to just keep bending down all the time, to pull my baby out from under.

Escalating my frown was my baby's penchant to pick up anything & everything lying around. She would pop it right into her mouth- without a second thought, in a swift fraction-of-a-second-movement, before I could even gasp in horror.

And thus, under this safe-zone table, she took a lot of liberty to relish her taste buds.
I went 'Aaaaaaahhhhh...Don't!!' more often than I called her name, every day.

So, on one fine day, I decided to have mercy on my spinal cord and put her in a high chair, with the harness on. She cooperated well and played with the toys I offered her.

Then, after sometime, she looked at the denied table. Her eyes scanned it with a touching desire. And then came the masterstroke - She turned to me and accentuated her eyes into those of a pitiable Bambi-deer, with a pout-plea on her lips. I was so defenseless in front of her now; she knew she owned me.

Out of her harness, she went crawling about the under-table-maze, the second I put her down!

I could literally see a backache coming in my direction with her strides, but it was worth seeing the explorer-start of a maze-runner in her.

The happiness in my eyes made me guess this is how one can paint a mother's love for her child – more for the life outside of her than for the life within her heart.

FOURTEEN

The other parent

Whenever somebody is addressed as a parent, the word 'Mother' comes to mind, more often than not.

Since it takes two-to-tango, this is the story of 'The other parent' – 'Daddy Dearest'.

It is difficult to put into words, the role a father plays in the life of an infant child.
Honestly speaking, this role is practically non-existent compared to a mother's postpartum responsibilities. But that's just a new mommee boasting, whose life has turned literally upside down.

Like many young mothers, I too went through a phase of blaming and envying my husband.
He was free from a tattered sleep, the dark-circles under my eyes, the never-ending fatigue in my body and the bi-hourly breastfeeding cycle, not to forget the liberty he enjoyed going back to work just days after becoming a parent.

It is less severe for some mums, whereas absolutely hard for others, wherein they sometimes feel like a single parent, despite having their husband by their side.

It is no wonder then that 'Mother' is akin to 'Parent', rather than 'Father'.

But this story is about the time I decided to look at my husband's role, as a father, through the magnifying lens.

Spoiler alert!
I was humbled by the vision.

This story is about the day my labor started, because that was the beginning of our parenthood.

There are multiple accounts of the strenuous hours of a mother's labor, told and retold, to glorify (and rightly so) the tremendous pain that a mother goes through for her child.
And it is true that childbirth is the most difficult experience in a woman's life, right before the most amazing one enters her life.
But, if involved, the father goes through a strenuous time too. His lady love is just a few hours away from gifting him the second, or even first some would say, love of his life - their child.

As I reminisced about my baby's birth one fine evening, I recollected that I wanted to stay fit (not slim, but healthy) during my pregnancy, for the benefit of a healthy child. For this, I joined a prenatal yoga class.

This class endowed me with physical & mental strength for both, pregnancy and labour. My husband participated in all the parental-activities including labor-role-play and even hypno birthing sessions, in this class.

But all this practice got tested when the labour pain struck hard.

On the day of my delivery, I was in immense pain (obviously!). While I thought all strength of mine would fail to cope up with the testing phases of labour, my husband came to my rescue.

He surprised me with what I never knew I would need.

While I was busy doing yoga through all of the months of my pregnancy, he was working on the essentials needed for the final day.

Yes, I was the one who made the labor-bag, packing in things for my newborn baby & myself. But what calmed me down during this 12-hour long labor was a playlist of relaxing music that my husband had created beforehand.

While chirpy on my good days, I was in no mood to even talk that day. Surprisingly though, my otherwise-at-a-loss-of-words husband had a ton of stories ready to humor me.

Although active during all of my pregnancy, I couldn't even move from side to side in the face of contractions on the day of labor. Here, he encouraged me to walk in the hallway, as he held my hand and watched me squirm in pain, being supportive as a wonderful dad-to-be.

I realized something really touching that day. To experience pain is bad, yes. But to see your loved one struggle hard in such pain, that too for hours without relief, while everything you do to help them falls flat - that vicarious pain hurts really bad too.

I asked him not to come into the labor room. He had seen me wince enough.
Although unsure at first, I was happy with this decision later as I was screaming at the top of my voice in there.

After half a day of labor, when I finally delivered our baby, he rushed into the room and took her in his arms. As the glow of having become a father radiated all over his face, he caressed my forehead and shared our baby with me along with a hug. I was overcome with all the joy possible in the world.

I have always believed that a mother has a more active role to play, especially during the early years, in a child's life, more so due to biological endowments. I am guilty of flaunting this a bit in my husband's face too.

But reliving the day of my child's birth always reminds me of how my husband went through his own phase of labor pain - one that I shall always respect him for.

I was aware of this - while I was screaming in the labor room, he had tears in his eyes outside (He never told me this himself).

Thankfully, they turned into tears of joy after our daughter entered into the world.

Be it a mother or a father - every involved parent has his share in this journey called parenthood. My child's father played his part while I played mine.

FIFTEEN

The BIG ONE

I found myself a little out of words on my baby's first birthday.

In all terms, literally & figuratively, time had just flown by since I had first held her in my arms. With her first birthday around, I started searching for birthday ideas. I was blown away by the number of stories available on the internet. At the same time, it was delightful to see such happy faces of young babies, whose giggles sparkled on their smooched face sandwiched between their loving parents.

There is so much that a parent wants to say to their heartbeat-like-child; through fancy letters, quoted caps, notes on balloons, decorative clothing, pictures on social media & even some dedicated recitations. This is one such story of a mother who wants to put a colorful frame around the birthday gala of her darling baby. The story of 'The Big One'.

So far, I had tried, to the best of my ability to capture the glorious first 365 of our days, through words, sounds and pictures. But this being the day of her BIG ONE, I wanted to register something all the more special than what we had treasured so far.

At the stroke of midnight, I looked at her, sound asleep beside me while I struggled to write something special, over simply observing all of her innocence. But seeing a child sleep makes a mother more aware than ever of how magnificent the rise of love in her chest feels like.

With the thought of her first birthday being round the corner, I started reaching the point where the violent gush of emotions became too strong for words to bind. All of the memories of the year gone by came racing back and it became too much for a single moment or a single breath to hold.

Hearing her first cry in the operation theatre.
Experiencing the twining of her one-day-old, cottony fragile palm around my gigantic-looking finger.

Caressing her gentle face, pacifying her after she had received her first vaccination sting at a tender one-month of age, as I struggled to hold back my own tears over her painful cries.

Seeing her three-month old lips turn into a mysteriously enchanting smile, in her sleep.

Wincing as I sniffed the odor of her soiled underwear, just seconds after I had put my five-month-old girl in my lap.

Looking at her hand reach out to me, touch my face and melt away all of me into the bliss that is 'she'.

Through all of these moments & many more, I started living all of the year gone by, all at once, right there & then.

It was overwhelming!

On the day of her birth, a year back, I went through the best day in the life of a woman – a woman who now gets called 'Mommee' by the cutest voice in the world.

While we will celebrate my girl's birthday every year, in fond memory of that one day years ago, no cake or candle will seem as wonderful as reading & reliving these moments over & over again.

Jot down your thoughts

SIXTEEN

Just turned ONE!

Grandma's cutie cupcake,
Grandpa's apple-of-the-eye,
Daddy's little angel,
Mommee's honeybun -
Look who just turned ONE!

The loudest radio,
The softest snore,
The cutest plea,
The messiest fun -
Look who just turned ONE!

Many a sleepless night,
Many a tiresome ache,
Many a dirty diaper,
Many a last-minute-run -
Look who just turned ONE!

Basket of giggles,
Box of troubles,
You are my one and only.
Like you there shall be none,
Look who just turned ONE!

SEVENTEEN

The unclicked pictures

Like every parent, I have clicked innumerate pictures of my baby.
Whenever my girl did something out-of-the-blue-adorable, I would spring up to my feet to fetch the camera (more often than not, the cute deed would have ended by the time I found the said lens.)

But this isn't the story of an adorable-to-death-picture-worthy-of-featuring-in-an-advertisement-baby-photo. This is a story of a picture, or rather all the pictures, that did not get clicked - 'The unclicked pictures'.

Here's the thing – my baby never really cared for the camera. So if I were to ask her 'Sweetheart, look into the camera! Smile, baby, smile!', TEN TIMES, she would glance in my direction ONCE, and then get back to throwing things around, as she were before.

As much as I find this annoying (because it makes my back hurt trying to get a decent click, even after hours of persuasion), I absolutely adore this aspect of my baby, too.

The reason is two-fold:
1. I see the epitome of 'Being Oneself' in her.

She is not who she is for the sake of a camera around. She is so, for her own self. There is just no fake in a baby.
She doesn't pout to get clicked or smile wide when she hears 'Say cheese!'.
She doesn't choose a background to look prettier nor does she edit the picture afterwards.
Unlike a grown-up, whose innocence left them as childhood did, she is the beauty of the waves on a beach as well as the serenity of silence in the hills: that is to say that she is nature at its best, meant for admiration without filters.
2. Her nonchalance towards getting clicked makes me live in & enjoy that moment to the fullest!
When I am not obsessed with running to get a camera, I get to extract louder laughs from the both of us, by tickling down that moment even more.
This leaves all of the gorgeous moments, wherein I wish I had a camera but did not, etched in the deepest part of my heart.

Words may get lost.
Pictures may fade away.
But these memories will always stay with me, like a gift to cherish forever.

I have bought many toys & books for my girl; many gifts have I lovingly showered her with but these 'unclicked pictures' are her eternal gift to me.

They are bigger & deeper than any gift I have ever received. They are mine in a manner nothing has ever been - Precious beyond the scare of stealth. Hers & mine. Always & forever.

EIGHTEEN

Khul Ja Sim Sim

This is a story about a daunting, yet important, experience of my life.

It's about the time I was facing a really challenging task at work. I had worked for quite some time in my life to say this - in all of the jobs that I had been assigned, none had been so hard.

With my recent promotion, I had been given very little time to finish Herculean tasks, multiple times in a day. It used to take a lot of brainstorming to come up with the perfect approach to please my insatiable, new client.

But that's not the hard part, yet. It was when this client dismissed my presentation with a frown, that I started to get agitated.

I submitted a fresh proposal, multiple times a day. These were all well-thought-of and thoroughly researched to suit the best of my client's needs.

Is it clear yet what this story is about?
Maybe saying in baby language will help?.

With my new promotion, every morning, I started the laborious task of going to Ali Baba's cave to try to open it. Only here, I was trying to put the gold inside, rather than taking it out.

Get it?
No?
Okay, some more details, perhaps -
I chanted 'khulja sim sim" twenty-odd-times, but the door to the cave didn't open.
I tried the fancier-English-version and pleaded 'Open Sesame' with style. The door didn't budge!

Sounds relatable, yet?
I tried singing all the rhymes that I know, but in vain.
I even made clown-like-funny faces but all I got was a cute-laugh with no acceptance of my gold. I tried to squeeze in the treasure while the cave laughed, but the minute I inched closer, it shut right back.
I tried opening it with all my might, but Good God, it didn't even crack open!

Tired and frustrated, I took a bite out of my gold.
It tasted fine so I shouted with a frown "This isn't that bad, why wouldn't you take it? It is so good for your health!"

No response. Complete & utter silence.

I decided to give up on donating the gold. It was gold after all, why shouldn't I have kept it for myself, I wondered. So I put the gold in front of me and started eating it, making yummy-yum sounds as I did so.

Professionally put, the promotion to becoming a mother added the most difficult role to my designation. Like every mother, I found my baby to be an obstinate client, when it came to eating good food.

Baby-way-speaking, my cute little gummy bear seemed awfully strong in refusing healthy food. She would eat anything other than what I placed on her plate.
Like, anything other than that!

Here is where the bulb in my brain sparkled bright!

Aaaaah...so she will eat anything but what's on her plate, right?

So I decided to bring a NEW plate and put the gold (her food) in it.
As I started to eat this food (now seemingly mine to claim), all of a sudden she developed an interest in it. She stretched out her tiny, slender neck to glance at what lay on my plate.

As I nibbled on small bites of the meal, she started pointing at it with a wishful desire of wanting to eat.

"Huh? You want this? Okay…"
I kept my fingers crossed, as I slowly put a small portion of food from my plate into her mouth.

Aha!
The cave opened!
I pushed in the treasure with joy dancing all over my face.

Task one - completed successfully. Hurrah!
The client was happy and so was I.

I felt so relieved.
That was until a thought crossed my mind -

'Next task is up in 3 hours'.

My victory dance slowed down.
I sighed and started brainstorming from scratch, again.

Thanks to my baby, I felt like an eight armed goddess & a red nosed circus clown, all at once.

Life with a baby, simply put, is - difficult in the moment, and super-fun in retrospect!

Jot down your thoughts

NINETEEN

Back to work

I used to work, more out of home than from it, before my baby was born. I took a break from it for some months, like most mothers do, post childbirth.

A short span of a few days of her naughty and adorable infancy was enough for me to realize that being with her, i.e. doing laborious work for her in the form of washing her unending load of soiled clothes, changing her diaper every hour, pacifying her inexplicable cries as well as being her night-time-vigil buddy, was way harder than any impossible-to-achieve-deadline-project I had ever taken up in my professional work.
My respect towards as well love for my mother has only multiplied after having become a mother myself, as I was now in the same boat.

This story, as such, is dedicated to all the 'Back-To-Work-Mommees'.

My little girl used to need me every minute, when awake, during the first few months. This amounted to almost all of my day going by her side as she refused to sleep. It left me awfully fatigued but it also gave me a sense of conceited joy that my child sought me.

As she crossed month after month of developmental growth, her 'need' for me decreased whereas her 'attachment' to me increased, thanks to the increment in her cognitive ability.
But I had to resume work some time, not just for my own self but also for setting a good example in front of my kid. I wanted to send out the message that no matter what, no matter who you are, you should always find time to do what you like. In this case that would be my vocation – "Do what you love and you shall never have to work", but I deviate.

So, back to work -
When I rejoined work, another difficult chapter started to unfold in my life.
On the first day of back-to-work, I expected to find myself lost in my child's worry, unable to concentrate on work at all.

And, don't take this the wrong way, but that did not happen.

In fact, I was so thrilled about working on things besides household & baby-chores, that I hardly got any time to miss my infant. I was constantly aware of the fact that we were apart, but not enough to be sad about it.

I started to wonder if I was a bad parent!

How could I not be missing my baby?

In order to berate myself, I called home a couple of times to check up on my girl, so that I would feel low. But she too was all right back home and this just added to my woes – 'Was she not missing me either?'
Now, this drove me further down the pile of pouting sorrow.

As the clock ticked, I kept recollecting her schedule:
"Now she must have woken up from sleep."
"Now she must be playing with her toys."
"Now she must be eating her snack."

Without consciously realizing it, I went right where I thought I wouldn't - into the 'missing my baby at work' zone.
I opened the photo-album in my cell phone and kept looking at her pictures right from the day of her birth up to the day.
'My sweet, little, darling daughter,' I muttered to myself. I missed her so much. But she seemed to not miss me.

That hurt...

An hour later, my cell phone rang.
It was from home.
I frantically answered it with 'Is she okay?'

'She is all right, just seems to be missing you. She has been really quiet all day and is looking for you everywhere.'

A sad and sadistic feeling rocked me into an alert state of
'I am going home right now!'
I rushed through the traffic, clicked open the door and saw her.

She jumped with joy at my sight.
I ran up to her and hugged her for a long time.

Blissful. That's how I felt.

I did not "work" work that day, but it still felt like a day well lived, no, really well lived.
As the days passed, we grew better at working apart - she, at home, and me, at work. But our moment of reunion at the end of every working day remains the same. This bliss, we are not parting with.

TWENTY

Nostalgic keepsakes

As the days go by, I am left wondering how & why the months of my baby's infancy had to slip by so fast - almost like grains of sand from between our palms.

I know. A clichéd sentiment.
But it is one strong sentiment.

As my bub grew up one tenth of an inch every single day, some things got left behind her, along with bucket loads of nostalgia associated with them.

This is one such story. A story of some 'Nostalgic keepsakes'.

I stumbled upon a 'blast from the past' box some days ago - A box filled with my baby's old clothes that, no matter how little my girl still was, did not fit her anymore.

I knew I had to give these clothes away, for a charitable cause. After all what use was a tiny romper to any grown up?

But before that, I had to do something else first.

I had to hold every single garment in my hands, inhale my baby's fragrance from its fibers, hug it tightly to my chest and let its not-so-heavy-weight weigh substantially on my heart.

I never realized that this would be an immensely tough goodbye to say.

As I took out the clothes, one pair at a time, I started to reminisce about the good old memories of my infant child in them.

A cute frock I could not help but buy, despite its daunting price tag, which she wore just twice, after which it never fit her again.
A sock whose twin got lost ages ago.
A romper my baby spoiled with curry, the stains of which have left stubborn traces behind forever.
The mittens my girl had chewed half way through, while going through teething.
The shirt with bunnies, looking like my little one, on it.
The bib she spent more time taking off than wearing.
The soft night dress that she slept heavenly in.

Call me a sentimental fool, but I shed a couple of tears, knowing that as wonderful as these memories etched in my heart were, those times were never coming back.

And if that much of nostalgia wasn't enough, I stumbled upon an onesie - the first onesie in her closet. It was a gift from a friend, when I was merely 4-months pregnant.

Now here is something we can all laugh at - When I opened this first gifted onesie, I had experienced two really strong feelings. One was that of heart-shaped bubbles bursting in my eyes at how adorable this handkerchief-sized clothing was. Second was that of disbelief over how anyone, no matter how tiny, could fit into a dress so small. I mean, it was barely the size of my two palms placed one above another!

It took me 5 more months to see how marvelously the onesie wrapped around my darling's little body. I loved it so much that I got her almost 10 more such cute onesies, thereafter!

All of these were now lying in this box, as she had grown out of them in no time.
Although I had clicked over a thousand pictures of her in them, to cherish for life, it was still hard to let go of something so precious.

So I have decided to keep a pair or two of these for memorabilia.
They have the mesmerizing scent of her beautiful infancy.

I naively wish this scent lasts in them forever, just like my love for these will.

TWENTY-ONE

A mother-daughter dance

Festivities.

Oh, what fun times festivities bring along with them!

In many cultures, these involve grand gatherings, delicious spreads, peppy music & lively dancing.

I like the last bit most of all – the dancing. And dedicated to that love, is this story. The story of a 'Mother-Daughter dance'.

Living in a vibrant country like India, and that too, residing in the heartland of the dance festival of Navratri (Gujarat), I grew up to be a Garba enthusiast.

Dressing up in an elaborate manner, dancing all night long with music chiming loudly to keep our energies high, night after night for nine long nights – nothing qualifies better for a dance festival to go to!

Now, this zest of mine took a hit when I became pregnant. As you may know, it is ill advised for an expecting mother to go dancing around with a baby in the belly.

Many a sacrifice has been made by mothers across the globe for their little ones, but during the high-on-the-emotional-horse-phase of my pregnancy, this sad piece of information brought a waterfall down my eyes. It was hard to forgo something I so dearly loved.

But, I did what I had to.
I put my strong face on and waited for the next year to come in the hope that I would live the leftover days of my passing youth then.

I can't help but wonder if my baby was witnessing all this emotional drama, from within me, during that time. If she was, then I am sure that she must have been thinking "So you think you will go dancing all night, while your 4-month old baby stays quietly at home? Hahahahahahaha!"

Yes, well, she would have been right.
Another year came and went by with my tears flowing again, this time under the pretext of postpartum blues.

But the year after that?
Oh, yes!
That one was going to be my year, finally!
My little girl was about a year and a half old and could run around without much supervision.
So I let my hopes run sky-high.

I joined a dance class to warm up my inactive-for-two-years-body.
I set aside some beautiful traditional ghaghra-cholis.
I started practicing my dance-steps at home every chance I got and I even sang garba songs as lullabies to my baby!

But from what happened next, I can say this with confidence:
"When man (Mommee) proposes, God (baby) disposes".
It is nature's way of saying 'Ha! Burnnn!'

What can I say? As it turns out, thankfully (or maybe not) my girl turned out to have my dancing-genes.
After the first time that I put on the traditional songs and skipped a few sassy steps to it, my daughter's quick learning, combined with her flair for dancing, kicked in.

Picture this, if you will: I am doing my dance practice and a minute later I realize that my baby is clinging to my leg, chiming "Mommeeeee, Mommeeeee".
With no choice left, I pick her up & start dancing with her in my arms.
She seems to enjoy this.
I smile at her bubbliness, as I sway her from side to side.
This feels nice; really nice.

I have never felt more in love with my dancing partner. The glee on my child's giggling lips is beautifully charming.

But, this now meant that I couldn't go out and enjoy the festivities of dance nights like I used to.
This now meant that my daughter's dance-fervor would supercede my Garba-fever, as my silly girl wouldn't let me step out of the house, to dance, without her.

Surprisingly though, wherever I took her along she ended up giving me the best of memories by running everywhere around and in between the circles of people dancing; observing their steps and trying to emulate the dance. More often than not, she kept falling down in the middle of a round-and-round dance step.

What can I say?
I have never enjoyed dancing more.
Now, I can't wait for the next year to come, where we will go dancing in a mother-daughter-twin outfit!

I do realize that, even then, it will be more of my little girl dancing around everyone and me running around her.

But that's the beauty of motherhood. I find that everything I would ever want or things that I never had, were with her and in her.

Just like I re-found my love for dancing in the happiness of her grooves.

I had naively thought that this was going to be my year. As it turns out, all the years to come are never going to be mine either; they are now going to be better by being ours.

And that is entirely MY bliss!

Jot down your thoughts

TWENTY-TWO

The first 'I Love You'

"I Love You!"

I say this to my toddler every day. I say it many times over, and I say it with complete honesty in my words.

Being a mother, I can't help it.

Toddlers are such an adorable bundle of cuteness that mothers tend to become struck with sugary-syrupy streaks in their hearts.

And it keeps getting better with every passing day as the kiddo keeps on learning something new, which inspires more and more love-filled 'awwwwws' from the love-struck mommee.

This story is about one such new thing. The story of my child's first 'I Love You'.

As I hugged my little girl with a good-morning kiss, her tight hug around my chest made the upcoming day seem like a welcome breeze.

I asked her the routine questions.

"Who is my strong girl?"
She softly replied with "I am."

"Who is my favorite bub?"
"I am."

"Who is my happy baby?"
"I am."

"Mummy loves you to the moon and...?"
"Baaaack!" She replied with the widest smile.

I was overjoyed with her response. I kissed her a thousand times over to the point where she had to push me away.

"Awwww...But I love you, darling..."
"I am."

I laughed so hard at this robotic, yet hilarious, reply from my toddler!

"Oh, Sweety!" I said trying to speak from between my mirth, "When I say 'I Love You', you say - "Love you too!' What do you say? You say - I love you too!"

She looked at me with bewilderment for some time, probably wondering why she had woken up to such a schooling session.

Nevertheless, I was persistent.

"Say, 'I Love You Too', baby! Say na...!"

After much coercing, she finally said

"I too too!"

"Wha…?" I asked.

"I Too Too!"

I did not know when to stop laughing for quite some time after that.

It is so delightful to listen to a young child's version of the sentences that we speak so mundanely - a pleasant break from which is this walking-talking entertainment channel in the form of my little girl, who I will always love too too.

TWENTY-THREE

Post weaning blues

My daughter was 22 months old, when, one day, my chest felt really heavy.
I don't mean this metaphorically.

There was something that I had to get off my chest - my breast milk.
But I couldn't.

I had just stopped breastfeeding my little girl.
And I had never felt lonelier.

This is the story of my post weaning blues.
A story that only a mother will possibly understand.

A mother starts to feel her baby within her womb since they are barely a heartbeat.
They slowly grow to tickle and kick the mum, day and night, in an annoyingly adorable manner. And then, after birth, they leave behind a beautiful design of drawings around their mother's waistline that people see as stretch marks.

For me, it was difficult to let go of my newborn baby, as I had never really thought of her as my daughter but considered her part of me. She was, in every possible way, mine. And then, after the cord was cut, she wasn't anymore.

My only consolation was the blessing of being connected to her through breastfeeding.

It is funny to realize now, how it looked like a task back then. I had to nurse my baby every few hours at first - not to mention the bi-hourly feeding at night. I recollect looking like a zombie with those red eyes popping out of my face; oozing with the fatigue of sleeplessness.

But then, a new mother's routine circles around her baby.
And so, befitting the role, I got to sleep only when my little munchkin slept.

Oh, how I used to wait impatiently for her to fall asleep!
This is how –

She used to fall asleep in my arms during the course of breastfeeding.
Tired and groggy of sitting and nursing for so long, I would hum to bring in her sleep sooner. But, after she fell asleep, I, surprisingly, would forget all the fatigue I had.

I would just keep looking at her face, tracing every line of her tiny body with all the love in my eyes. It felt magical to feel this connected to another human being.

What hurts now is the thought of never being able to feel as heavenly as that with her again.

I tried to cheer myself up through welcoming the world on my palate.
For as long as I'd nursed my girl, I had to arrange my entire diet around her needs. This is because a major source of nutrition for the baby is mother's milk, given its unmatched benefits.
So, in order to make sure that my child got the best, I had to cut down on all of my caffeine and other unhealthy food like spicy or fried items, any road-side food (which can be delicious at times) and even abstain from noodle related food preparations as they could have sauces that are not advisable for babies.

With a diet restricted to healthy items only, I used to dearly crave everything forbidden.
How funny is it that now that I could consume anything I wanted, I didn't feel so great about it!

Was this because I was bothered by the heaviness in my chest?
If so, then why did the ache inside my heart feel greater than the one outside it?

I wish I could explain it, but I can't.

The only word that language seems to have developed to describe what I was experiencing is "post weaning blues", but this knowledge of experiencing a common phenomenon didn't soothe the longing that I felt so miserably for my child. That she cried for want of my milk all through this weaning-off phase, only added to my hurt. I hugged her and apologised, all along, till she was fine with this.

With the desire to preserve those precious moments of nursing, I availed a breast-milk-memoir-jewellery, in the form of a pendant.
I will gift it to my girl, once she grows up.

Till then, I will wear it close to my heart.
Maybe, its touch will instil some of the bliss of breastfeeding in my heartbeats again.

TWENTY-FOUR

A twisty toddler

Some time ago, my baby grew out of her infancy and entered an interesting phase of being a toddler.

And it goes without saying, that she pretty much started functioning as a toddler as well. That is the essence of this story. The story of 'A twisty toddler'.

Which is to say -
She kept running around everywhere without any purpose.

She felt tempted to do everything I had said not to.

She threw more things than I had the energy to bend down and pick up.

She ate food not just with her mouth, but with her entire face, her hair, her limbs and even her clothes.

She'd act adorably dramatic till the point I took out the camera - in front of which she wouldn't pose even for the sake of her favorite treats!

She would hurt herself quite a few times during the day, and then would wait for my expression to tell her whether to cry or not. If I went "Aaahhhhh, what happened?!", then she would know that a loud, painful wail was appropriate. And if I looked the other way, then she would consider the fall to be a bubble-burst at best and continue jumping around like a monkey.

She also became pretty good at the whole toddler-cry-acting-thing with the flair to let out a bawl one minute and then emit a soft chuckle the very next second.

She did cry for real upon waking up & not finding me around, which I, as a young mother, selfishly found heart-warming.

But what I found most adorable about this 'toddlerhood' of hers was her ability to completely alter the pronunciation of any word. While she repeated everything she heard, it was her bubbly touch to regular words that made them sound exotic.

'Mommee' & 'Papa' were quick for her to catch, but, soon after, she began experimenting with the dialect.

The early ones were as expected.

Water was 'Mum mum' to her.
Food was 'Khaikhai'.
Bath was 'Naayinaayi'.
Sleep was 'Neeni'.

Ball was 'Boo', and so was a book somehow.

All of these, she spoke with a giggling happiness all over her face.

Perhaps it was my crazy laughter, but every time she chose to add her gibberish touch to words, she would giggle & repeat that same word thrice. Every time.
Or maybe, toddlers are instilled with a magical cuteness from above, to bless their parents with repetitive fun.

Either way, my girl seemed to love twisting animal names the most, and here are some of my favorites from her baby-dictionary:
Dog was 'Bhaubhau'.
Cat was 'Meow'.
Gorilla was 'Gogiya'.
Squirrel was 'Turio'.
Elephant had been cutely nicknamed 'Elin' for the sake of convenience.
Lion was 'La yawn' (She made an animal sound French!).
And for some bizarre reason, Fish was 'B'. That alphabet doesn't even appear in a fish's name!

But there is no winning against a toddler hell bent upon eliciting more and more laughter out of her mother, is there now?

And it was amidst this loving laughter that I realized something -
I know that as a parent, I am supposed to be teaching things to my toddler.
Ideally, I should be correcting all of her silly, misspelled words.

But….nah!
I consider her language far superior to anything else that the world is used to.
Her ways don't follow any rules.
They are as independent as they are original.

Additionally, given how I can understand every weird sentence she forms using this language (All hail Mommee super powers!), I consider it to be our secret code for life.

Eventually she will learn the adult version of words.
But as she does so, I hope she doesn't forget her cute version of this language called 'Baby'.

I know I never will.

Jot down your thoughts

TWENTY-FIVE

Just another human being

I confess to being weak, at times.
I confess to being selfish, at times.
I confess to losing my temper, every now and then.
I confess to shedding the superwoman tag, as well.

I confess to being human, and not an eight-armed magician.
And I also confess to being satisfied with being human.
And so this story is just about that. A story about 'Just another human being'.

I love my kid to the moon and back. I have said this a thousand times over and I will say it again that many times more during the course of this life.

But no matter how I wish that my universe would revolve around just my child, I do engage in other activities too, similar to other human beings.
And hence, just like an average person, I too am prone to fatigue and mood alterations, based on the day.
It could be as small as some misdirected anger or as tough as an excess of workload – either way, I end up feeling worse than I do to begin with, for what I end up doing around my kid.

On bad days, I end up yelling around the house.
It is in those days that I like myself a little less.

My little girl is always her happy-go-lucky self, thanks to the rosy bubble of her innocent childhood

And then comes in one of my bad days.

She would be hopping & jumping around like any other day, asking me to play along, which I try hard to accommodate.
But after some time, my exhaustion takes over and I end up responding with what she dislikes – "Not now, baby...I am really tired!" with a yell.
As expected, she doesn't understand these words from the dictionary & continues to be clownish by beeping my nose, pulling my ears etc.

I try really hard to explain this to her but she doesn't budge.
She remains true to her jolly nature.

I wish I could do that too, because this is where my shout goes beyond a yell into becoming a full flared howl!
She gets taken aback and looks at me with those big dewy eyes, wondering why I'm being so cold.
I can't make her comprehend my state, so I request again, with a plea.

How a child inherits the environment around her comes into play here when she reacts with a head bang.

Not being a big fan of head bumps, I tend to push her away, and at such points, her angelic eyes well up. This being an imperfect world, such incidents happen with a young mother at times. It breaks my heart every time such an event occurs with my child.
Every single time.

I have promised myself that I would never repeat this, and have always let her in with a tight hug.

That is, until I have a bad day again, which is when my promise gets tested. I've even broken it sometimes. And I have been dissatisfied with being just a human being, then.

But as much as I would like to not lash out at my child, my outbursts have only increased with the passage of time. That is because with age, my child's naughtiness has also grown.

It is not just about being tired anymore.
It is about the fact that when I see my child do something improper, I experience the need to correct her; and the best way to gain her attention, at times, comes with authority in my voice.

It is also about the fact that no matter how big a space my child occupies in my heart, I have other things on my mind too. In order to be a part of this world that goes beyond the two of us, I need her to understand the state that my body is in, as opposed to the jovial state of her mind.

For a long time, it was hard to not see myself as a big, old yeller-kind-of-mother, because honestly, that's how I feel society judges young mothers like me. But I realised that I wouldn't want to fool my child into believing in a perfect world.

I will be her friend more often than not, but there will be days where I will have to be my own friend before being hers.

Yes, I will probably have to monitor the decibel level of my voice. sAs long as I communicate this aspect of my human nature with my child, all will be well.

TWENTY-SIX

Uh-Oh!

I feel like some motherly-feelings are universal, like I don't want my baby to ever get hurt.
But then, I cannot always protect my child from getting hurt either.

If a part of me feels happy seeing my little one run, then the other part must brace for her falls too.

There are ways to prepare oneself for a smoother run in life, though. Choose a safer path or wear protective armor while sliding down the adventurous one.

But, for reasons better left unjustified, I can't talk about these to a toddler.

For my bub, it was either the offer of a consoling hug after she got hurt or no rough play at all. The former would mean letting my heart break every time she cried and the latter would mean robbing my love of a good childhood.

So I devised a third way - moderation in my response after my child's inevitable fall.
But I am not talking about saying 'Bad Floor' by hitting the ground she fell upon.

I am talking about a story of 'Uh-Oh!'.

Every time something fell (my girl or her toy, either way), I started saying aloud "Uh Oh! Did something fall? Did you hurt yourself? Are you okay?", all the while offering a comforting hug.
And Voila! She did not cry or punish the ground over getting hurt. If anything, she would now express if, and how, she was hurt.

It was a good tactic.

After the first few times, my girl caught on to the "Uh Oh!" really well.
I heard the 'Uh Oh!' when she dropped a toy.
There was an 'Uh Oh!' when she spilled food from her chair.
There was even an 'Uh Oh!' when she bumped her head against something, but never was there a cry anymore.

It seemed that she was gaining strength & confidence with every 'Uh Oh!'.

And so, a few days later, I did not get alarmed upon hearing an 'Uh Oh!', from the room next door.

"She is fine. She will just get up & dust herself off.", I said to myself.

A minute later, she came up to me and pulled my dress. She was 1/5 the size of my height. My dress's edge was all she could reach.

She pulled me in the direction of the other room saying "Mommee, chalo (Come Mommee)".

I followed her with curiosity.

When I entered the other room, she left me standing at the door, walked up to the couch, pointed at the gravy she had spilled all over it and said “Uh Oh!”

I was speechless.
My jaw dropped a few inches.
And, I was speechless.

The laughter that followed, though, lasted a few weeks, as I told & retold this tale to everyone.
But I couldn’t make myself say “Uh-Oh” without a deep pause, ever again.

TWENTY-SEVEN

A little, yellow duck

Quack, Quack!

I laugh out loud, every time I hear this.

While there isn't anything particularly funny about a quack, what is hilarious, although, is this memory built in my mind over a deep friendship between my toddler & her favorite toy - 'A little, yellow, rubber duck'.

This toy is hugely popular amongst cute little ones, who for some reason need an equally cute bathing companion for themselves, in the absence of whom bathing them becomes more like wrestling with them for the mother.

So when my toddler received a gift of bathing ducks, her joy knew no end.
Given her adorable, todder-ish lisp, she fondly called these 'Kuck' or 'Kucky'.

And yes, it sounds really funny, but cute at the same time.

One time, as I made my baby get ready for her bath, she was quick to recall that her new friends were missing. She stepped into the bathing area and with a swift turn and asked 'Kucky?'

I heard her, but was a little down with morning-routine-fatigue due to which I chose not to respond, as that would have required me to get up and fetch a small duckling from her toy chest.

She was determined, though.
"Mommee, KUCK!"

I had to give in.

"Yes, baby, okay...I will get your Kucks!" I said, as I got up with a touch of an old lady's bones cracking within me.

Time was merciful as I found them quickly and presented them to a now-radiant-with-joy-girl of mine.

As she played with her 'kucks', I sat down beside her and picked up one small rubber duck myself.

It sat comfortably on my palm as I wondered at the marvel of human art - with tiny black eyes, a pouted beak, puffed up wings and a squeaky base, this little rubber duck was indeed as cute as a button.

I faintly recollected being obsessed with one such duck-toy of my own, when I too was a child; only then I adored that duck like my life depended on it.

As I remained lost in nostalgic memories of a childhood that now seemed to belong to another lifetime, my baby caught notice of my aloofness.

"Mommee...Kucky..." she said pointing towards the one in my hand.

"Huh?" I replied, still lost.

"Kucky, Mommee...Quack, Quack!"

At first I gaped at my child with an open mouth.
And then, about two seconds later, I burst out laughing.

She had to emphasize with the quacks!
She had more adjectives for something she now probably presumed her elderly mother wouldn't understand.

Or maybe just like my little self, she too wanted this toy that her life (or rather bath) depended on so dearly; something I held onto, as she patiently waited for my reflection to end and her bath to begin.

As I gave her the requested 'kucky' back, she threw it alongside the other ducks in the bathtub, only to climb in with them a second later.

As the splash-games began, so did my long lost childhood in front of my eyes.

Whatever time of the day, whichever activity it may be, being a part of my child's 'babyhood' is like living mine all over again, only this time there are two of me.

Jot down your thoughts

TWENTY-EIGHT

Unconditional love

I recently saw a photograph that I completely related to.

It was that of a mother holding a baby in her arms, just as the baby is getting ready for a shot of vaccination. The doctor stood holding the needle just inches away from the curious-yet-unwavering-baby.

What made this picture absolutely touching was the fact that the baby seemed to be calmly looking at the needle about to pierce through her tender arm, quite unlike the mother, who had a wince on her face as she looked the other way. She was bracing herself for her child's incoming pain.

I have never felt anything so vicariously before.
It felt like watching my own self in a flashback to my baby's first vaccination shot.

This is a story on similar lines. A story of 'Unconditional love'.

Yes, it is true that a mother feels everything her child does, as I believe is true vice-versa. And so the child's glee reflects upon the mother's face, as does the child's agony.

Every man or woman is eventually on their own in life, but for as long as a kid wakes up looking for their mother, she is going to be the guardian angel for her baby, in good as well as in bad times.

Which is why, when it came to exhibiting tough love, the mother in me had to gather all the strength in my bones to stop myself from going weak in moments of need - which is maintaining a strict face while looking at the dripping innocence all over my child's face.

This comes to test particularly when I try to add a note of discipline to my kid's life.

I have accommodated many of my baby's requests, much against my better judgment at times. Expectedly, I have more often than not, regretted doing so.
For example, when my baby caught a cold because I gave up on trying to make her wear a cap against her will, or when she ate everything other than the healthy meal, I made only for her to get a bad stomach-ache the next day, I had a long face-palm expression.

It is such occurrences that have made me firm in the face of my little girl's stubborn requests, over time.
I am told that this is called 'Tough Love'.

It allows you to feel your child's pain, but it also has you standing strong at the same time.

What I wasn't told was that this tough love would make one's child turn their face away from the mother or, worse, make them draw favorites from the family (anyone who offers what the mother restricts is an eligible candidate)

Sadly, on one occasion, when my girl showcased anger at my strictness, by not coming to me, this streak of tough love hit my heart with pain.

I begged her, trying to make a naive toddler understand why green vegetables were better than potato chips.

She did not see eye to eye with me.

We parted ways for the day on this sour note.

As I drove off to work that day, my feelings ached at the memory of the frown on her angelic face, despising my role to exhibit tough love.
I wished there were a better way to deal with a reluctant toddler, but nothing came to mind over the fatigue of having tried everything else for hours in vain.

As my baby slept that night with her frown intact, I apologized for having been rudely strict. I wanted to tell her how I could feel her pain, but I couldn't afford disturbing her sleep.

I repeated 'I love you' more times than I could count. Sleep did not come easily to me, still.

Thankfully, the morning came with some sunshine.

My daughter woke up with a cry.

Her father tried comforting her, but she cried and insisted on having her 'Mommee'.

I jumped up and went running to her.
It felt good to see my child seek her mother, over anybody else, in times of need. There was a hint of sadism in there, somewhere, as my husband looked at me drool with happiness.

As I wiped my girl's tears and let her head rest on my shoulders, my tough love seemed to fade away in the background of a life full of such hugs.

I will be exhibiting tough love again, for sure.
And my girl will also continue to pout or frown at my strictness.

I will scold her & she will get upset with me.
She will throw things around & I will get mad at her.

The cycle will continue so on & so forth.

But what will comfort me is the knowledge of a beautiful heart, beating with unconditional love towards me, within my child;
As does mine for her, no matter how much she tires me out with her refusals.

TWENTY-NINE

Lullabies & sweet dreams

As a child starts to speak, the initial days of the child's immensely cute, lisp-filled talk are enough to make the mother's heart grow twice its size within her joyous chest.

True to this, I swayed merrily when my little girl started speaking adorably.
Most of the time, I would just keep looking at her with a smile painted over my eyes.
Every mundane word she uttered made me feel like that was the first one to be ever spoken out aloud. Over these silly giggles, I would forget all of my troubles, big & small.

So, lost did I get in the wonder of her speech, that my baby had to, once, touch my face (rather tap my forehead) with her buttery palm to bring me back to our conversation, by repeating what she had just said.

But by doing so she put me back into the same trance of wonder again.

I knew I would be getting a lot of such moments for the next few months as she picked up sentences.

This story is about the time she picked up something wonderfully. This is a story of 'Lullabies & sweet dreams'.

I get really tired trying to keep up with the day's tasks, home or otherwise.
But making time for my baby's childhood is an important task as well.
After all the other tasks are done with, the night comes with a wonderful relief called sleep. But, just before that is when magic happens.

My little girl helped us develop a lovely routine of mother-daughter chitchat, in the name of sharing the day's details, bedtime stories & lullabies, right before we doze off. This was our little 'We Time' - or so I like to call it.
We started this night-time routine when my bub was barely a few months old.
Initially it used to be just the mother talking to a barely attentive infant.
Little did I realize that she was paying full attention!

A few nights ago, when I started to get drowsy after over an hour of bedtime sweet talk with my baby, she tapped my cheek gently to wake me up, as it seemed against routine for her mother to fall asleep before she did.

I opened my eyelids with a lot of effort. As lovely as this talk-time of ours was, a lengthy day tends to get the better of a mother.
After having sung my daughter's favorite lullaby for the tenth time, I asked her to go to sleep. When she did not, I couldn't help but close my own eyes.

So, when she nudged me to wake up, I repeated, "Please go to sleep, baby. Mommee is really tired. Please let me sleep, darling".

She understood that I was tired & sleepy.
In fact, she understood it so well that she came near my face, kissed my cheek like I do to her at bedtime, ran her hand over my head and started to sing the same lullaby to put her mother to sleep!

In the shimmer of night-light across her face, a delightful innocence beamed in her eyes.

I doubt the gasp of 'Awwwwww' in my sigh was audible beyond the sound of my heartbeat.

I wanted to grab her doll-like body & dance all over the place!

But my girl was bent upon mimicking her mother to perfection.

"Mommee, eyes, close!" she said with an enchanting lisp, as her index finger pointed decisively towards me. I chuckled merrily & obeyed to welcome some sweet, sweet dreams that night.

As I caressed my baby's cheek, in sleep, for having turned the mother-child table around with a stroke of genius, she giggled with a pink blush and continued singing the lullaby.

A mother can never really know what her child will speak like. However, that the child's talks will be sprinkled with such colorful-childhood-confectionery is the unfathomable, yet surprising, promise of a babble.

THIRTY

A walking-talking, mini zoo!

Things are never white & black with the little human beings known as babies.
With them, everything is colorful.

This story pans over a long period of time, as opposed to covering any one incident of a mother's life.
Several times, I tried putting a title to it, but the content of this story kept changing every few days.

For a long time, my heart was set on calling this 'The Copy-Cat Effect'.
I switched to 'The Parrot In The House', later.
'My Little Monkey' caught my thoughts for a while too.
And then there was 'Tears Of A Small Crocodile', 'A Fluffy, Little Bunny' and 'A Teddy Bear In The Making' as well.

All these put together, my baby is my 'Walking, talking, mini zoo'!

I have found some or the other cute, little animal's reflection in her since the day she was born.
But she seems to have just perfected the acts, over & above appearances, over the years.

I was aware of the fact that a growing baby captures almost everything around her - the sights, the sounds & even the actions.
These, then, a baby replicates in a manner of exact imitation, which makes any mundane act either gosh-inducing or hilariously amusing.
It is because of this that I used to act consciously around my little one, lest she picks up a bad gesture or silly word thrown by me in a state of absent-mindedness.

Alas! If only one's mind could be tamed to such discipline.

Without intimation, my girl would pick up her father's office bag & declare that she was off to work.
Fancying her mother's mirror image, she would pick up some make-up to dab her face pretty.

With insistence upon 'I will eat on my own', she would make a mess out of the soup that she stubbornly ate with a fork, forgetting that, when her mother had used it, there were noodles on the plate. She copied everything with the zest of a cat, but with the silliness of an infant, all at the same!

This doesn't end here.

I would be on a phone call and realize a few minutes later how my bub was repeating everything I had said earlier.
Add to this the charm of her baby-ish lisp, and I could sit all my life by her side, listening to every word that came out of her mouth, draped in a silky, sweet cuteness, which sounded a tasteless-bland when I had said earlier it.

How does she do it?
She twists all adult vocabulary, adds her own flair to elderly actions, turns them into the miniature lens called 'adorable' that is she and emits it with rainbow bubbles popping all around it!

Let me not go there where I try to capture this melodious flair of her speech on a video – that is exactly when she freezes in front of the camera as if she were said 'Statue' to; that's another chapter for another story.

For now, her one-girl-zoo keeps adding one animal to its list of talents, every few days.

She is my copycat girl as well as my repeating-parrot.
This parrot is also a little monkey who keeps jumping up & down the last springs left in our couch.

That monkey often falls down the tired couch, hurting herself, not much, and crying out too much, with crocodile's tears flowing its cheeks.
As I wipe these tears and caress my baby's face, she falls asleep in my lap; I keep looking at the rosy cheeks & the peachy nose on my bunny-faced-innocent-little-child.
As I hug my girl just before I put her to bed, I realize how every soft toy in the world has been ruined for me by the cushioning effect of this teddy-bear pressed against my chest.

My everyday-visit to this mini zoo is a blissful journey that has been, and will keep on being, captured in my memory for life.

Jot down your thoughts

THIRTY-ONE

Walking on thin ice

Words are a really powerful medium to express oneself in. When used well, they can communicate one's thoughts & emotions in the best way - which is why I couldn't wait for my little one to start talking.

This story is a twin chapter from the events of my walking-talking, mini zoo. This is my side of the story, called 'Walking on thin ice'.

I did all that I could to emanate verbal responses from my child, in order to expedite her speech.
I spoke to her at length.
I read stories to her.
I informed her of all the events happening around us.
I enquired about her hunger, her mood and her wish to play.
I even used different languages for her to grasp varied dialects!

But, let's just say that the result was not what I had expected.

My baby started speaking early, which was great - so much so that now she wouldn't keep quiet at all!

With the power of communication by her side, my bub could now share what she felt or wanted. Now, there was always a chirp going on in the background of our house in the form of her sweet-lisp-filled-baby-talk.
Such was my girl's fancy for talking that when she couldn't get a response from me, she would engage in conversations with the birds flying by, with her inanimate toys, and weirdly enough, with her own self at times!

I actually happened to love these talks as anything that came out of her baby-mouth was cute as a button; but there were times when I wished she would keep quiet. Not for long but just for five minutes of pin-drop-silence.

Was that too much to ask for?
It seemed so to her.

Not only would she not keep mum, she started repeating everything she heard.

Everything!

I understood, and even admired, her fast-learning skills.
But I was coming very close to certainty that all babies have a naughty button in them, because from everything that I spoke to and around my baby, she

always managed to pick up the most inappropriate words.

I would say all sorts of positive, flowery, rosy things to her, but the minute I lost my mind over someone on the phone and blurted out "Are you insane?", she would be sure to keep on chanting "Insane! Insane! Insane!" all day long.

Needless to say, being around a baby is like walking on thin ice.
A young mother has to be really, really careful about everything she does or says as God knows what silly thing her child might pick up from her next.

Although, if I think about it, it isn't as bad as it sounds. I did end up trimming away a few loose feathers of mine - ones I am better off without – issues like trivial anger, unsuitable language, poor choice of mannerisms and even sloppy expressions. These "issues" - once the habit of my youth - were going haywire, now that I was on my way to becoming a responsible adult.
If my baby is to learn anything from me, then like every mother, I too wish to for her to take after the best side of me.

This would mean that now, I would have to do without any of the carefree habits that I myself was not proud of.

This isn't what I had anticipated, as a young mother, that in the process of trying to raise a good human being, I would find myself becoming a better person too.

I believe it is alright to walk on thin ice, then.

THIRTY-TWO

Big deal!

Time sprinted away as we (my baby & I), played peek-a-boo.
So fast was its pace that I did not get to blink my eyes twice before it was time for my baby to start preschool.

While still small in the way of needing my help with daily tasks, she suddenly became big enough to be on her own.

This story is about one small step my baby took into her playgroup, and the big impact it had on my heart. It's a story of a 'Big Deal'.

As a mother, I am used to receiving unsolicited advice from everyone.
People say, "It's no big deal! Your kid had to step into an institution some day, right?"

Right.

Every baby grows up one day.

Every toddler enters school, sooner or later.

Every kid becomes a student in a few years.

And then, every child grows into a pubescent adult ready to move on to new terrains, away from the nest that once nurtured their childhood.

And as I capture this journey of decades in a few lines, this deal seems to be sitting pretty heavily on my chest, making my breath feel like a storm inside of me that could burst with tears any minute.

I am getting emotional, yes. That's because this is a big deal for me.
Ironically, I spent months waiting for this to happen - waiting to get some time for myself, once my girl started being on her own, even if it was just for a few hours every day.
But, my baby's absence was not only making my heart grow fonder, it was killing me slowly with a flood of sensory memories of her - one glimpse at a time.

I used to wonder, back when I wasn't a mother, as to why mothers seem so confused over issues concerning their children. They seemed to have a hard time getting their priorities straight between what their heart wanted and what their mind did.

Needless to say - given how my feelings are now torn between choosing from the two halves of my own self - me & my child, the wonder has subsided beneath my love as a mother.

I'm not going to say that I will always choose my baby, despite always wanting to.
I will have good days, and then I will have some not-so-good days, because life is not a bed of roses; and because a mother is not gifted with the superpowers she desires.

That is why, knowing that some days will make me seek some time away from my child, only to get back into being the best version of myself in her interest, is still a painful process.

With my girl taking her first step towards her separation from me, comes the beginning of a new trial for us. We are finally crossing the bridge to being independent, independently.

It's no surprise, then, that this is how we will keep playing peek-a-boo for life, with the intervals of the hiding become longer as the years go by.

And that is exactly what makes this a big deal.

THIRTY-THREE

I wish I knew

As I dropped off my baby on the first day of her pre-school, I felt really unhappy with myself. The teacher had to tear her away from the hug that she so tightly held onto.
I felt like I was a kangaroo and that she was the baby in my pouch, whose time to face the world on her own was being forced onto her, much against her will.

As I drove away from my wailing baby, I started wishing for a few things. This is that story of 'I wish I knew'.

To begin with, I wished I knew why I felt gloriously sad and lovingly touched; both at the same time, over my darling's call for her mother.
But, over anything else, I quietly wished for her to have forgotten about me as she entered the class, because the thought of her crying, red eyes that searched for her mother inside was tearing me apart from within.

Next, I wished for the hours to clock away as fast as the first few years of my little one's childhood, so that I could experience her warm hug around me again, soon.

But as time took its own sweet time to pass, my mind wandered to other memories of my toddler's adorable infancy, with thoughts such as,

I wish I knew where the twin of her cute socks went. Till date, it's a mystery unsolved.

I wish I knew why she relished a food item one day and then absolutely rejected the same dish when I made it a few days later.

I wish I knew why she picked up all the silly words I unconsciously said around her, without showing any signs of remembering all the good things I consciously tried to make her learn.

I wish I knew how she manages to lose all the toys she plays with in completely opposite corners of our home.

I also wish I knew why banging things, throwing them from a height and crushing them beyond repair is the only way my toddler knew how to play with a toy.
Then, I wish I knew how she managed to outgrow all of her dresses labeled 6-12 months by the time she was 10-months old.
And then again, I wish I knew how at times a dress labeled 12-18 months fit her fine at the age of 2.

I wish I knew where she derived those cute, magical eyes from - eyes that could melt my anger in seconds no matter how big a mess she had created.

I wish I knew where this side of me was; a side capable of being so head-over-heels-in-love with the stupidest of things my munchkin did (things I found less than amusing, when somebody's child did it, in the past).

I wish I knew what kick she got out of doing exactly what she was asked not to!

As the pile of my wishes kept growing with my lost thoughts, time did what it does best.
It passed.

I found myself waiting for my bub to come out of her preschool, absolutely sure that she would have been an inconsolable mess inside all this time, given how I'd left her.
That is when she took me by pleasant surprise - she came out fine, and her face donned an angelic smile the minute she saw me.

I ran out to collect her.
Her hug around me again was precious!

As I hugged her all the way back home, I wished I knew where she gets this amazing gist of childhood from - the unexpectedly surprising strength of smiling back to normalcy, after having been through tough times.

I knew that she may cry the next day as we tore apart again.
But for now, my bucket list of wishes was more than full, as was the contentment in my heart.

Jot down your thoughts

THIRTY-FOUR

What a father feels

Most of this book is filled with experiences shared between my child and me.

But this story is not really about us. It is about a chapter from the parallel journey of parenthood that my partner-in-crime, my child's father and my husband, has experienced with me. This is a story of 'What a father feels'.

This is about the time we took a trip with our little girl. We travelled to distant lands, tasted new food, awed in the majesty of scenic beauty and then ran around our toddler's impossible-to-stay-at-one-place-feet through foreign towns.
It was a lot of fun.

Like any doting parent, I wanted to capture these sweet memories in my camera, and so I did. In the last leg of our trip, I was looking at what I had managed to click through the past few days.

The pink in those drooling lips on my shoulder,
The chase my baby had with pigeons in an open street,
The excitement in her eyes when her father offered her ice-cream for the first time,

The placid look on her face as she slept in her father's arms,
The funny laugh she exhibited at her father's pranks around ancient statues,
The happiness on her father's face as he swirled her around a fountain...

In that moment, I realized that there were hardly any pictures of me.
Her father had overshadowed my presence, literally, in the camera roll.

So, later that day, when her father asked me to take yet another picture of him with our little girl, I did not hesitate to show my displeasure at being missing in action.
So, it happened that he stood beside a beautiful bridge, holding our sleeping girl close to his heart, just like he had done during most of our trip, only now he faced a rant from my side.
"Why are there so many pictures of you, and so few of me? You did not get many pictures even with me on our honeymoon! And now, all of a sudden, you are getting your pictures clicked left, right, and centre?" I hissed.

He replied with the utmost form of genuineness.

"I don't know how big she would become the next time we travel. Maybe she would not want to be in my lap for so long then. Maybe she would sleep in her own seat, rather than on my chest. Maybe she would prefer walking on her own, rather than holding my finger. Maybe she would have outgrown being this toddler I hold close today."

I bit my lip to stop the tears from building up in my eyes.

I looked at the floor and then rolled my eyes to gain back my composure.

"Ummm...I don't think the light is good in this direction...why don't you...ummm...stand here, instead?" I said, as I dragged him by his arm.

And then, I clicked many more pictures of the two of them.

I always knew my little girl was growing up.
I just never realized how fleeting the days of her childhood were.

Her father's honest-to-heart-reply was one glimpse into his side of the parenting lens - It went on to tell me that what I am registering through words, he is perhaps doing through pictures.

And if pictures could tell stories, then my husband has prepared a trunk-full of them just like I have with ink & paper.

THIRTY-FIVE

Hide & seek

When I look at my child, I know that this world was created with pure intentions.
And then to look back at myself makes me wonder where those intentions got lost in the process.

No, I am not indicating that adulthood makes one impure.
I just feel that it makes one lose the charm of purity that we are all born with.

In this regard, I want to talk about the power of innocence through a story of 'Hide & Seek'.

I look at everything around me through the colored lenses that the world has rubbed on my eyes.
My young child, on the other hand, has a clear mind and a trusting heart.
She is full of innocence and devoid of worldly hues.

The other day, I entertained her through a game of hide & seek.
I asked her to close her eyes & count to ten.
She did (well, at least she tried to) count to 10 but got lost at finding what comes after 4 – after which she simply jumped to shouting "Ten!".

I suppressed a hearty laugh, lest it gave away my hiding spot.

She started calling out "Mommee, Mommee..." thinking that's how the game works – I hide and then just come out upon being called by a happy, clapping toddler who prides upon having busted my hiding spot.

But since it doesn't work that way, I did not come out and let her search some more.

When she finally found me hiding behind a door, her ecstasy knew no bounds! Her giggle made my heart beat joyously as well.
I hugged and congratulated her on the big win.
And then just as she was about to close her eyes to stir the resting-in-peace-soul-of-the-person-who-invented-numbers, I held her hands and asked her to hide instead.

This is where I did not see what was coming.

Before I could get to count one through ten (correctly that is), my little girl hid herself under a quilt.
She put a quilt, on her head, right in front of me!

I stood there watching this – My little child, sitting in the middle of our bed, with her body draped completely within a quilt. It was like looking at her in plain daylight. It was either that, or the quilt had grown awkwardly big & protruded from different sides.

This time, I did not suppress my gigantic laughs.

She did not give away her cover yet, and moved the quilt from over her head – with one eyebrow and half of an eye looking at me, at which point, my laugh only turned into a stomach-aching-teary-eyed laughter riot.

If innocence were to embody itself into being, this is what it would look like.

My child's world is so simple!
Everything is 0 or 1, white or black, nay or...oh, it is mostly nay to everything these days, but that's another story.

My world, on the other hand, is not so simple. It has a lot of greys.

Looking at my young child, I believe I know how God intended human beings to be – simple & pure at heart, with faith in everything.

But as life happens, time seems to differ.

Time doesn't heal.

It alters.
I guess that is why I am an altered version of my baby-self.

But my girl's baby-hood is still here, so I will make the most of it, vicariously that is.
After all, she isn't hiding anything from me, anyway!

THIRTY-SIX

Guilt at midnight

A mother is always divided between being the responsible adult that the tasks of the day require her to be and being the happy-go-lucky-carefree-side-of-a-mother that her child seeks from her.

Now, I entertain my baby's ideology of chuckling over nothing, most of the day.
I let her eat in between intervals of her running-relay, as my patience gets tested alongside her meal going cold.

I watch & support her as she throws around toys across the house, pushing away thoughts of an impending task of collect-and-collate-the-toy-box from my mind.
I even cater to her whims & fancies as she expects me to become a jester one minute and an animal-mimic the other, just to put her to sleep.

But I get tired much faster than my little one does.
And in this state of exhaustion, I am in no mood to run around her, let alone run with her, to plead tasks out of her.
So, if she does not listen at this point, she gets to see the dark side of me – a side which doesn't hesitate in yelling at her.

I make myself believe I do nothing wrong, as disciplining a child is a part and parcel of good parenting.
I have even succeeded in getting past the adorable pout on my baby's face as she attempts to cry at being scolded.

But, as time takes the day into the night and she falls asleep, I am hit with an image of the red devil sitting on my shoulder - the one who made me lash out at my angelic baby.

This is, thus, the story of 'Guilt at midnight'.

With my girl sleeping in a heavenly manner and soft light falling on her face, all of her cuteness and innocence becomes ten times magnified.
This just makes my guilt dig a deep hole in my heart.

"How could I be this cruel to such a darling child?"
"Why did I have to shout at her?"
"I made these dainty eyes experience showers of pain."
"I am not a good mother..."
"I am sorry, my love..."
"I love you so much...I am so sorry..."

I try to hold her close to my heart without disturbing her beauty-sleep, as I plant a thousand kisses on her face…

I am odd, I believe.
I am the bad cop as well as the good cop, both in one person.

Something tells me that every mother is such, in some way or the other – oddly torn between her heart and her mind, with regards to her child.

As this guilt grows to a peak at midnight, I wish my child wakes up to the better side of me, a side devoid of any anger.
But, I know that raising a toddler is challenging enough to make this easier said than done.

I can only hope that my little baby registers all my love in her sleep, far more than she remembers my yelling in my bad times.
As for my guilt at midnight, I hope it gets replaced by calmness in daytime as time goes by.

Jot down your thoughts

THIRTY-SEVEN

Copy that!

It feels great when somebody tells me that my girl takes after me, and then not so much when I'm told that my child is a replica of her father.

Yes, I like to believe that all of this cuteness that I adore in my daughter has its roots in me.

But, this story covers the aspects that I did not know I had for her to copy.
This is a story of 'Copy that!'

I often look at my little girl's face and at a picture of my childhood and say, "She is like my twin!"
I observe the sprouting ponytail on top of her head, and I recollect how my father called mine a small 'shaving brush'.
I see the way she pouts her lips and I become the smug mother with "Yes, that is exactly how I did it."

But it only came to my attention a few days back, that in my bub, I see everything that I want to.
What I mean to say is that I have been so involved in trying to establish a direct link between little me and current her, that I did not realize how she takes after my present-day-self as well!

A few days back, we were out with family, for dinner.

My father passed over something to me, to which I said, "No, thank you", and got on with my conversations within the group.
The very next minute, he passed the same thing over to my toddler, and her reaction was this elaborate:

She tilted her head upwards, so as to throw her hair back.
Pushed her arm out, perpendicular to her chest.
Closed her eyes.
Bobbed her head from side to side.
And then, drew her lips into a 'Noooooo'.

I looked at her and laughed.
Just when I was laughing heartily, my father said something that put a sudden break on my mirth.

"That is exactly how you did it!" he said.

"What?" I asked in pure disbelief.

"Yes, that is exactly the way you did it. She copied you to perfection!"

I looked at my dad, and then back at my child.
She had the most ordinary, innocent expression on her face, with no hint of mischief.

"Noooo! I did not express myself like that! I simply said 'No'. That was it. Nothing more."
My parents laughed at my being so defensive.
Herein, my girl laughed as well, which made me question my stand.

Ever since that day, I have become extremely conscious of my baby's expressions and actions.

She acts in a dramatic way, at times.
Now, it is possible that she is training in theatrics without my knowledge, but as remote a possibility as that is, she could also be simply copying what she observes in her parents.

I would like to pin this on her father, but deep inside my heart I know who the drama queen in our family really is.
And so, every time my kiddo enacts something in a vivid manner, I am left wondering how and when I expressed myself like that.
But more importantly, I wonder if my daughter was laughing in the background at my thespian acts, just like I laugh at hers now, saying "Copy that!" in her mind.

It looks like we'll never know.

THIRTY-EIGHT

Weapons of defense

A well-behaved child is every mother's dream.

What I mean by 'well-behaved' is that the child may jump around and play for a while and then obey when asked to stop by a tired mother.

I need not explain why this is a dream.
Nevertheless, in order to make this dream come true, a mother puts in a lot of effort into teaching good manners to her kid.
I did too.
What I did not do is foresee the story of 'Weapons of defense' unfolding.

I followed all the chapters in any good book:
Say 'thank you', when given things.
Say 'sorry', when you break the said things.
Pick up your toys after you are done playing.
Don't throw the toys in the garbage after you are done playing.
Give Mommee a 'good-morning', as well as a 'good-night' kiss.

I am glad to see my child picking up most of these pretty well, except for 'picking up her toys' part.

She says thank you and sorry in the cutest possible manner.
And she always plants the softest kisses to begin and end my day right.

But, I never knew that these etiquettes would find utility in her weapons-of-defense-box. Yes, every toddler has a quiver full of customized arrows, only to be used in times of need.

Over a period of time, my girl seems to have gauged the importance of her adorable gestures in my life, and ever since then, has not hesitated in using them against me.

So, for every time she commits a blunder, i.e. break a toy, spill water all around, spoil her clothes or scatter all my cosmetics yet again, she is quick to be ready with a charming 'Sorry, Mommee'.

It works like a charm I just cannot scold her over that lovable look on her face.

But, every weapon loses its power over time, and so, the effect of this 'magical sorry' faded with the fifth toy that she broke.

So, this time, she upped the dosage with an immediate kiss on my cheeks after the cute sorry. I kept looking

at her, wondering whether to worry about the new pair of clothes she had just ruined or to just go "awwwwww" and kiss her right back.
Needless to say, I did the latter without the blink of an eye.

But then, as this effect started to wean off too, my little girl went for the kill with an immediate tight hug, over having smashed my lipstick all over her face.
I wanted to scold her - I really did! But, she wouldn't leave her hugging hold around my neck.

It felt good to have her heart beat against mine, but that was an expensive lipstick to let go! I had to shout at her in order for this to not repeat.

When I finally managed to break her grip and bring her face-to-face with me, instead of berating her, I ended up in a teary-eyed-laughter.

In front of me lay her lipstick-covered-face, with colored arrows running from her lips to her eyebrows. She laughed along with me, from behind these lines, like an adorable clown, and the moment got what it needed from both of us - some more memories to retell in future.

No matter how many weapons of hers get put up and then nullified in defense, she always manages to find the ultimate "Cupid's arrow" of her childish charm that will never lose its endearment to the mother in me.

THIRTY-NINE

Trick or Treat!

Every child has some memory of each of these formats:

a. Being berated big time, when they act naughty

b. Being coerced big time, when they act stubborn

This is a story of a variety of phenomena dealt with by mothers through tricks & treats of their own. A story of 'Trick or Treat'.

Given the limited number of hours a day presents a tired parent with, dealing with a child with nothing but a smile of one's lips seems like a task even Gods would find difficult to accomplish. So, simply put, a child can be managed easily through the allure of a candy or through the fear of scolding.

I, for one, have many, many such memories of my childhood (being scolded more often than being coerced!).

But times have changed, and with them so have the methods of dealing with a child's tantrums. A parent is expected to be gentle all the time. There cannot be any sort of yelling or shouting.

The sweet side of a parent is expected to keep flowing like a melted-chocolate-fountain!

According to a new theory, a child can be made to bring out their best behavior through just positive reinforcement.

Do you want to know what that is?

It is an (almost) impossible-to-implement rule of being nothing but polite to your child; even in the face of the worst of their mood-swings as well as in dealing with their temper-tantrums, whether they are being stupid or being stubborn; during their best behavior as well as their worst - A parent ought to be as cool as ice.
To a young mother like me, this theory struck as being devised by somebody who, by some miracle, had been blessed with a trained kid (I mean trained to behave well, no matter what) or by some miracle, had a superpower of emotion-control.

Any parent, besides these two categories will tell you that little ones can be impossible to sway at times, no matter what positivity you infuse in your words & actions.
But I do like the idea of getting a child to agree without any yelling, so I would like to put my faith in this theory. But for that, I had to be creative in my

approach, as patience is not really a young mother's strong suit.
Since the tried & tested method of 'Carrot Or Stick' model has fallen into disrepute, I had to devise my own version of something I like to call 'Trick Or Treat'.

Now, I love talking to my young child.
Having a strong conversational bonding is the ultimate wish of any parent.

However, one cannot expect a little toddler to understand their mother's helpless fatigue over their own staunch desire for something like a need to go play in the park at midnight; or perhaps their crazy unwillingness to get out of the car when coming back home from a drive.

As trivial as these problems sound, they are indeed a challenge.

Hence - Trick Or Treat.

'Trick' is the distraction I used to take my baby's mind away from her stubbornness.
This can be a simple "Oh, the monkey took away the box of cookies...Look there he goes!" as I place them behind my back with a swift move of hand. Or it could be a "There are more such cellphones like Mumma's in the other room; go find them!"

'Treat', on the other hand is the weak side of the mother in me, who promises my girl of indulgence in things of her choice, if she were to accept things of my choice, in return. "I promise to take you to the park if you eat broccoli" or "Please finish this activity in my hand first; how else can I give you a candy?"

I don't know how these paint me- good or bad. Personally, I prefer to be termed 'Tactful'.
But I am a tired, biased mother, after all.

And in the interest of full disclosure here, I need to tell you how not foolproof this gimmick is –
My girl has, more often than not, found the box of cookies behind my back. And funnier still is the fact that when I asked my cell phone back from her then she put her hand behind her back with "The monkey took it away, Mumma!" thus giving me a bittersweet dose of my own medicine.

So, here's the honest revelation - I am not so fond of these gimmicks. But, as long as time & energy in me permits, I try to even things with my toddler through conviction.

For all the other times, there is always 'Trick Or Treat!'

FORTY

A New-Year-Resolution

I saw this conversation in a television soap-
A man tells his colleague that his wife is really attached to their baby; so much so that if they hadn't cut the umbilical cord then the mother would still be clinging onto their child!

Funny, I know.
But, do I completely relate to that man's wife? Oh, yes!

I don't know, though, whether to laugh over this or mull at how crudely the world judges a mother's affection towards her baby.

While I may not qualify as the mother who never let her umbilical cord get cut, I certainly am attached quite strongly to my baby. She has spent more time in my arms than in her cradle.

In the first few months after her birth, despite complaining about the same, I did not spare a single chance to hold her.
I think I loved it as much as I loved sighing over it.

This is because being with her was like being with myself - aside from the fact that there were two bodies to feed & clean now. Still, I wouldn't bat an eye away from her face, fearing she might give me the cutest smile in that one microsecond. Over the course of time, I have only struggled to squeeze all other work into the frame around my baby's childhood.

I guess that is why, to a naive bystander, a mother may look like a selfish person, wanting more of her baby & more of life at the same time.

Well, nobody else will understand this selfishness of a mother, but a mother. This is one such story. A story of a 'A New Year Resolution'.

As would be expected, this was around the New Year. As another year went by, I was filled with a strange, yet pressing, feeling of nostalgia.

While I have never really been attached to days or dates, it was a big hoarding that caught my eye that day, as I was driving past it.

It said '2019' in big, bold letters.

I couldn't understand why this simple reminder of a new year hit me so hard with all the days of the year gone by. I believe I was finding it somewhat difficult to cope with the fact that a full year had gone by with time filling in the gap between my hand & my baby's growing fingers.

I wasn't ready to let go off her tiny hands, yet.
I wasn't done relishing the living-giggling-radiance that was my 2.5 feet tall, walkie-talkie girl.
I yearned for many more hugs, as she ran into my arms after having been separated for too long. I couldn't do without the warmth that filled my heart as we cuddled into sleep every night.

I guess, I wasn't prepared to stop being this happy version of me that I felt every day, no matter how busy or tired my hours seemed. And with the year on the calendar telling me that those days were numbered, I wanted to hold onto the sand of her childhood in my hands, all the more firmly.

Does that make me selfish? The man in the soap would say so, wouldn't he?

Well, let him! Let all silly men like him be!

With such acceptance, I decided that this was my New-Year-Resolution
"I resolve to be selfish this year-

Selfish for being delighted with the softest of kisses that my infant daughter has now learnt to shower upon me, every time she realizes Mommee is getting mad; Selfish for wanting to see what new surprise awaits me at the end of the day, all thanks to the 'I learnt a new trick today' spree of my little girl;

Selfish for newer words that spring out of her mouth, as she twists each one into a honey-suckled dialect of her own, making me laugh to no end!;

Selfish for more sleep now that she has chosen her permanent sweet-sleep-spot in my chest with my arms wrapped around her wherein I get the feeling of having her back within me, all over again!

I do not know of any more ways of saying this - I love my baby.

And I am going to continue doing so selfishly, in all of the years to come, and then in many more beyond that.

Happy new year to the Mommee in me!”

Jot down your thoughts

Jot down your thoughts

www.ingramcontent.com/pod-product-compliance
Lightning Source LLC
Chambersburg PA
CBHW050012170726
48282CB00025B/377